Anonymous

The Book of Knowledge and Guide to Rapid Wealth

1000 facts worth remembering

Anonymous

The Book of Knowledge and Guide to Rapid Wealth
1000 facts worth remembering

ISBN/EAN: 9783337248369

Printed in Europe, USA, Canada, Australia, Japan

Cover: Foto ©Lupo / pixelio.de

More available books at **www.hansebooks.com**

THE BOOK OF KNOWLEDGE,

AND

Guide to Rapid Wealth.

1000 FACTS WORTH REMEMBERING.

NEW YORK:
STREET & SMITH, Publishers
31 Rose Street.

Entered according to Act of Congress, in the year 1891,
BY STREET & SMITH,
In the Office of the Librarian of Congress, at Washington, D. C.

CONTENTS.

SECRETS OF THE LIQUOR TRADE.
  Cider without Apples ; Cider Champagne ; to Neutralize Whiskey ; Port Wine; Maderia ; Sherry ; to Correct Bad Taste in Wine ; to remove Ropiness ; to restore Flat Wine ; to restore Sour Wine ; Ginger Wine; Brandy; French Brandy; Pale Brandy; Cognac ; Bitters; Gin; Schnapps; Rum; Whiskey; Arrack; Beer; Root Beer ; Ginger Beer ; Spruce Beer ; Old Beer; Mead; Stomach Bitters; Soda Syrup; Bead for Liquor; Coloring for Liquor; Wax Putty; Cement for Bottles. 3–11

DRUGGISTS' DEPARTMENT.
  Arnica Liniment; Cherry Pectoral; Balm Gilead; Blackberry Cordial; Brandreth's Pills; Bronchial Troches ; Pulmonic Wafers; Candied Lemon ; Camphor Balls ; Camphorated Oil; Camphor Tablet ; Camphor Eye-Water; Canker Cure ; Cephalic Snuff; Cure for Pimples, Eruptions, Etc.; Cure for Headache, Neuralgia, Etc. ; Chamomile Pills ; Chlorine Pastiles ; Cholera Morbus; Cholera Cure; Corn Cure; Cough Compound; Cure for Diarrhœa ; Digestive Pills ; Disease of Bowels; Dried Herbs; Dysentery; Anti-bilious Pills; Pain Extractor; Godfrey's Cordial; Female Pills ; Hydrophobia Preventitive; Infant's Syrup; Ointments; Tincture for Wounds; Tonic, Whooping Cough; Cure for Drunkenness 11–19

MANUFACTURER'S DEPARTMENT.
  Indelible Ink; Imitation Gold, Silver and Honey; Vinegar ; Soap ; Cements ; Paints ; Roof Composition ; French Polish; Oil for Furniture; Glue; Inks; Blacking; Copying Paper; Plating Fluids; Amalgams; Bronzing; Metals, (tempering); Varnish...................... 19–36

TOILET, PERFUMERY, ETC.
  Hair Restorers ; Rouges ; Face Washes ; Pomatum ; Tooth Paste; Cologne; Cold Cream; Cosmetics; Dandruff; Essences; Eye-Water... 36–43

FACE PAINTS... 43-44

HUNTERS' AND TRAPPERS SECRETS.................. 44-46

FINE ARTS AND SCIENCES.
   Transferring; Potchiomoni; Embalming; Wax Flowers 46-48

FARMERS' DEPARTMENT.
   Potatoes; Killing Vermin; Horses........................... 48-51

CONFECTIONERS' DEPARTMENT.
   Ginger; Peppermint; Clarifying; Twist Candy; Taffy; Fruit; Pop Corn; Icing; Saffron; Chocolate; Lemon, 51-54

HOUSEHOLD.
   Alum; Yeast; Fire Kindlers; Insects; Lye Colors; Preserving Meats; Quick Growth of Vegetables; Drying Corn; Restoring Scorched Linen; Remove Stains; Pickling; Mending broken Ware; Preserving Milk; Vinegar; Cleaning Silver; Water-Proof Cloth; Cleaning Furniture; Washing; Burns; Smokey Chimneys; Turner's Wood; Removing Paint; Fence Posts; Milk Test; Mending Tinware; Removing Stains; Wet Feet; Moth Destroyer; the Butterfly; Poultices to remove Grease; Bleaching; Purifying Water; Chemistry of Lead; Preserving; Prevent Freezing Eggs; Fly Paper,... 54-73

DYES FOR CLOTHS,... 73-74

DYES FOR BONES AND IVORY............................ 74-75

MISCELLANEOUS... 75-82

PRINTING INKS,... 82-85

HORSES.. 85

GENERAL RECIPES... 86

THE BOOK OF KNOWLEDGE,

AND

GUIDE TO RAPID WEALTH.

SECRETS OF THE LIQUOR TRADE.

Cider Without Apples.—To each gallon of cold water, put 1 lb. common sugar, ½ oz. tartaric acid, 1 tablespoonful of yeast, shake well, make in the evening, and it will be fit for use next day. I make in a keg a few gallons at a time, leaving a few quarts to make into next time; not using yeast again until the keg needs rinsing. If it gets a little sour make a little more in to it, or put as much water with it as there is cider, and put it with the vinegar. If it is desired to bottle this cider by manufacturers of small drinks, you will proceed as follows: Put in a barrel 5 gallons hot water, 30 lbs. brown sugar, ¾ lb. tartaric acid, 25 gallons cold water, 3 pints of hop or brewers' yeast worked into paste with ¾ lb. flour, and 1 pint water will be required in making this paste, put altogether in a barrel, which it will fill, and let it work 24 hours—the yeast running out at the bung all the time, by putting in a little occasionally to keep it full. Then bottle, putting in 2 or 3 broken raisins in each bottle, and it will nearly equal Champagne.

Cider Champagne. No. 1.—Good cider, 20 gallons, spirit, 1 gallon; honey or sugar, 6 lbs. Mix, and let them rest for a fortnight; then fine with skimmed milk, 1 quart. This, put up in champagne bottles, silvered and labeled, has often been sold for Champagne. It opens very sparkling.

Cider Champagne, No. 2.—Good pale vinous cider, 1 hogshead; proof spirit, (pale) 3 gallons; honey or sugar, 14 lbs. Mix, and let them remain together in a temperate situation for one month; then add orange-flower water 1 quart; and fine it down with skimmed milk ½ a gallon. This will be very pale; and a similar article, when bottled in champagne bottles, silvered and labeled, has been often sold to the ignorant for Champagne. It opens very brisk, if managed properly.

British Champagne.—Loaf sugar, 56 lbs., brown sugar (pale.) 46 lbs.; water (warm) 45 gallons; white tartar, 4 ounces. Mix, and at a proper temperature add yeast, 1 quart; afterwards add sweet cider, 5 gallons; bitter almonds (bruised,) 6 or 7 in number; pale spirit, 1 gallon; orris powder, ½ ounce.

Cider—To Keep Sweet.—1st. By putting into the barrel before the cider has begun to work about a half pint of whole fresh mustard seed tied up in a coarse muslin bag. 2d. By burning a little sulphur or sulphur match in the barrel previous to putting in the cider. 3d. By the use of ¾ of an ounce of the bi-sulphite of lime to the barrel. This article is the preserving powder sold at rather a high price by various firms.

To Neutralize Whisky to make various Liquors.—To 40 gallons of whisky, add 1½ lbs. unslacked lime; ¾ lb. alum, and ½ pint spirits of nitre. Stand 24 hours and draw it off.

Port Wine.—Worked cider, 42 gallons; good port wine 12 gallons; good brandy, 3 gallons; pure spirits, 6 gallons. Mix, Elderberries and sloes, and the fruit of the black hawes, make a fine purple color for wines, or use burnt sugar.

Madeira Wine.—To 40 gallons prepared cider, add ¼ lb. tartaric acid; 4 gallons spirits; 3 lbs. loaf sugar. Let it stand 10 days draw it off carefully; fine it down, and again rack it into another cask.

Sherry Wine.—To 40 gallons prepared cider, add, 2 gallons spirits; 3 lbs. of raisins; 6 gallons good sherry, and ½ ounce oil bitter almonds, (dissolved in alcohol.) Let it stand 10 days, and draw it off carefully; fine it down and again rack it into another cask.

Port Wine.—To 40 gallons prepared cider, add, 6 gallons good port wine; 10 quarts wild grapes, (clusters;) ½ lb. bruised rhatany root; 3 oz. tincture of kino; 3 lbs. loaf sugar; 2 gallons spirits. Let this stand 10 days, color if too light, with tincture of rhatany, then rack it off and fine it. This should be repeated until the color is perfect and the liquid clear.

To correct a bad taste and sourness in Wine.—Put in a bag the root of wild horse-radish cut in bits. Let it down in the wine, and leave it there two days; take this out, and put another, repeating the same till the wine is perfectly restored. Or fill a bag with wheat; it will have the same effect.

To remove Ropiness from Wine.—Add a little catechu or a small quantity of the bruised berries of the mountain ash.

To restore Flat Wine.—Add four or five pounds of white sugar, honey, or bruised raisins, to every hundred gallons, and bung close. A little spirits may also be added.

To restore Wine that has turned sour or sharp.—Fill a bag with leek-seed, or of leaves or twisters of vine, and put either of them to infuse in the cask.

Ginger Wine.—Take one quart of 95 per cent. alcohol, and put into it one ounce of best ginger root, (bruised and not ground,) five grains of capsicum, and one drachm of tartaric acid. Let stand one week and filter. Now add one gallon of water, in which one pound of crushed sugar has been boiled. Mix when cold. To make the color boil ½ ounce of cochineal, ¾ ounces of cream tarter, ½ ounce of saleratus, and ½ ounce alum in a pint of water till you get a bright red color.

Brandy.—To 40 gallons of pure or neutral spirits, add 1 pound crude tartar, dissolved in 1 gallon hot water; acetic ether, ¼ pint; bruised raisins, 6 pounds; tinct. kino, 2 ounces; sugar, 3 pounds; color with sugar coloring. Stand 14 days, and draw off.

French Brandy.—Pure spirits, 1 gallon; best French brandy, or any kind you wish to imitate, 1 quart; loaf sugar, 2 ounces; sweet spirits of nitre, ½ ounce; a few drops of tincture of catechu, or oak bark, to roughen the taste if desired, and color to suit.

Pale Brandy.—Is made the same as by the above recipe, using pale instead of the French, and using only 1 ounce of tincture of kino for every five gallons.

Cognac Brandy.—To every 10 gallons of pure spirits add 2 quarts New-England Rum, or 1 quart Jamaica Rum, and from 30 to 40 drops of oil cognac put in half a pint of alcohol, and color with burnt sugar to suit.

British Cognac Brandy.—Clean spirit (17 up), 100 gallons; high flavored cognac, 10 gallons; oil of cassia, 1½ ounces; oil of bitter almonds (essential), ½ ounce; powdered catechu, 10 ounces; cream of tartar (dissolved), 16 ounces; Beaufoy's concentrated acetic acid, 3 pounds; coloring (sugar), 1 quart or more. Put the whole into a fresh emptied brandy piece, and let them remain a week, together with occasional agitation, then let them stand to settle.

Brandy Bitters.—Bruised gentian, 8 ounces; orange peel, 5 ounces; cardamoms, 3 ounces; cassia, 1 ounce; cochineal ¼ ounce; spirit 1 gallon. Digest for one week, then decant the clear, and pour on the dregs, water, 5 pints. Digest for one week longer, decant, and mix the two tinctures together.

Gin.—Take 100 gallons of clear, rectified spirits; add, after you have killed the oil well, 1½ ounces of the oil of English juniper, ½ ounce of angelica essence, ½ ounce of the oil bitter almonds, ½ ounce of the oil of coriander, and ½ ounce of the oil of caraway; put this into the rectified spirit and well rummage it up; this is what the rectifiers call strong gin.

To make this *up*, as it is called by the trade, add 45 pounds of loaf-sugar, dissolved; then rummage the whole well up together with 4 ounces of roche alum. For finings there may be added two ounces of salts of tartar.

Holland Gin.—To 40 gallons of neutral spirits, add, 2 ounces spirits nitre; 4 pounds of loaf sugar; 1 ounce oil juniper; ⅛ ounce oil caraway. The juniper and caraway to be first cut in a quart of alcohol; stand 24 hours.

To reduce Holland Gin.—To 25 gallons pure Holland gin, add 25 gallons pure French spirit; ½ gallon of white sugar syrup; mix thoroughly.

Cordial Gin.—Of the oil of bitter almonds; vitriol, turpentine, and juniper, ½ a drachm each; kill the oils in spirits of wine; 15 gallons of clean, rectified proof spirits, to which add 1 drachm of coriander seeds, 1 drachm of pulverized orris root, ½ pint of elder-flower water, with 10 pounds of sugar and 5 gallons of water or liquor.

English Gin.—Plain malt spirit, 100 gallons; spirits of turpentine, 1 pint; bay salt 7 pounds. Mix and distill. The difference in the flavor of gin is produced by varying the proportion of turpentine, and by occasionally adding a small quantity of juniper berries.

Aromatic Schiedam Schnapps, to imitate.—To 25 gallons good common gin, 5 over proof, add 15 pints strained honey; 2 gallons clear water; 5 pints white-sugar syrup; 5 pints spirit of nutmegs mixed with the nitric ether; 5 pints orange-flower water; 7 quarts pure water; 1 ounce acetic ether; 8 drops oil of wintergreen, dissolved with the acetic ether. Mix all the ingredients well; if necessary, fine with alum and salt of tartar.

St. Croix Rum.—To 40 gallons p. or n. spirits, add, 2 gallons St. Croix Rum; 2 oz. acetic acid; 1½ ounce butyric acid; 3 pounds loaf sugar.

Jamaica Rum.—To 45 gallons New-England rum, add 5 gallons Jamaica rum; 2 ounces butyric ether; ½ ounce oil of caraway, cut with alcohol; 95 per cent. Color with sugar coloring.

Jamaica Rum, No. 2.—To 36 gallons pure spirits, add 1 gallon Jamaica rum; 3 oz. butyric ether; 3 oz. acetic ether; ½ gallon sugar syrup. Mix the ethers and acid with the Jamaica rum, and stir it well in the spirit. Color with burnt sugar coloring.

Santa-Cruz Rum.—To 50 gallons pure proof spirit, add 5 gallons Santa-Cruz rum; 5 pounds refined sugar, in ½ gallon water; 3 oz. butyric acid; 2 oz. acetic ether. Color if necessary.

Pine-Apple Rum.—To 50 gallons rum, made by the fruit method, add 25 pine-apples sliced, and 8 pounds of white sugar. Let it stand two weeks before drawing off.

Irish or Scotch Whiskey.—To 40 gallons proof spirits, add 60 drops of creosote, dissolved in 1 quart of alcohol; 2 oz. acetic acid; 1 pound loaf sugar. Stand 48 hours.

Monongahela Whiskey.—To 40 gallons proof spirits, add 2 ounces spirits of nitre; 4 pounds dried peaches; 4 pounds N. O. sugar; 1 quart rye (burnt and ground like coffee,) ¼ pound all-spice; ½ pound cinnamon; ½ pound cloves. Put in the ingredients, and after standing 5 days, draw it off, and strain the same, if necessary.

Batavia Arrack.—To 12 gallons pale rum, add 2 oz. flowers of benzion; ½ ounce balsam of Tolu; 1 ounce sliced pine-apple. Digest with occasional agitation for a month; then add ½ pint raw milk agitated well for fifteen minutes, and rack in a week, a fine imitation.

Rum Shrub.—Tartaric acid, 5 pounds; pale sugar 100 pounds; oil lemom, 4 drs.; oil orange, 4 drs., put them into a large cask (80 gallons,) and add water, 10 gallons. Rummage till the acid and sugar are dissolved, then add rum (proof,) 20 gallons; water to make up 55 gallons in all; coloring 1 quart or more. Fine with 12 eggs. The addition of 12 sliced oranges will improve the flavor.

Bourbon Whiskey.—To 100 gallons pure proof spirit, add 4 ounces pear oil; 2 ounces pelargonif ether; 13 drs. oil of wintergreen, dissolved in the ether; 1 gallon wine vinegar. Color with burnt sugar.

Strong Beer, English Improved.—Malt, 1 peck; course brown sugar, 6 pounds; hops, 4 ounces; good yeast, 1 teacup; if you have not malt, take a little over 1 peck of barley, (twice the amount of oats will do, but are not as good,) and put it into an oven after the bread is drawn, or into a stove oven, and steam the moisture from them. Grind coarsely. Now pour upon the ground malt 3½ gallons of water at 170 or 172° of heat. The tub in which you scald the malt should have a false bottom, 2 or three inches from the real bottom; the false bottom should be bored full of gimlet holes, so as to act as a strainer, to keep back the malt meal. When the water is poured on, stir them well, and let it stand 3 hours, and draw off by a faucet; put in 7 gallons more of water at 180 to 182°; stir it well, and let it itand 2 hours and draw it off. Then put on a gallon or two of cold water, stir it well and draw it off; you should have about 5 or 6 gallons. Put the six pounds of course brown sugar in an equal amount of water; mix with the wort, and boil 1½ to 2 hours with the hops; you should have eight gallons when boiled; when cooled to 80° put in the yeast, and let it work 18 to 20 hours, covered with a sack; use sound iron hooped kegs or porter bottles, bung or cork tight, and in two weeks it will be good sound beer, and will keep a long time, and for persons of a weak habit of body, and especially females, 1 glass of this with their meals is far better than tea or coffee, or all the ardent spirits in the universe. If more malt is used, not exceeding ½ a bushel, the beer, of course, would have more spirit, but this strength is sufficient for the use of females or invalids.

Cheap Beer.—Fill a boiler with the green shells of peas, pour on water till it rises half an inch above the shells, and simmer for three hours. Strain off the liquor, and add a strong decoction of the wood sage or the hop, so as to render it pleasantly bitter, then ferment in the usual manner. The wood sage is the best substitute for hops, and being free from any anodyne property is entitled to a preference. By boiling a fresh quantity of shells in the decoction before it becomes cold, it may be so thoroughly impregnated with saccharine matter, as to afford a liquor, when fermented, as strong as ale.

Root Beer.—For 10 gallons beer, take 3 pounds common burdock root, or 1 ounce essence of sassafras; ½ pound good hops; 1 pint corn, roasted brown. Boil the whole in 6 gallons of pure water until the strength of the materials is obtained; strain while hot into a keg, adding enough cold water to make 10 gallons. When nearly cold, add clean molasses or syrup until palatable,—not sickishly sweet. Add also as much fresh yeast as will raise a batch of 8 loaves of bread. Place the keg in a cellar or other cool place, and in 48 hours you will have a keg of first-rate sparkling root beer.

Root Beer, No. 2.—For each gallon of water to be used, take hops, burdock, yellow dock, sarsaparilla, dandelion, and spikenard roots, bruised, of each ½ ounce; boil about 20 minutes, and strain while hot, add 8 or 10 drops of oils of spruce and sassafras, mixed in equal proportions, when cool enough not to scald your hand, put in 2 or 3 table-spoons of yeast; molasses, ⅜ of a pint, or white sugar, ½ pound, gives it about the right sweetness.

Superior Ginger Beer.—Ten pounds of sugar; 9 ounces of lemon juice; ½ a pound of honey; 11 ounces of bruised ginger root; 9 gallons of water; 3 pints of yeast. Boil the ginger half an hour in a gallon of water; then add the rest of the water and the other ingredients, and strain it when cold. Add the white of an egg, beaten, and ½ an ounce of essence of lemon. Let it stand four days, then bottle, and it will keep many months.

Spruce Beer.—Take of the essence of spruce half a pint; bruised pimento and ginger, of each four ounces; water, three gallons. Boil five or ten minutes, then strain and add 11 gallons of warm water, a pint of yeast, and 6 pints of molasses. Allow the mixture to ferment for 24 hours.

To Cure Ropy Beer.—Put a handful or two of flour, and the same quantity of hops, with a little powdered alum; into the beer and rummage it well.

To give Beer the appearance of Age.—Add a few handfuls of pickled cucumbers and Seville oranges, both chopped up. This is said to make malt liquor appear six months older than it really is.

How to make Mead.—The following is a good recipe for Mead: On twenty pounds of honey pour five gallons of boiling water; boil, and remove the scum as it rises; add one ounce of best hops, and boil for ten minutes; then put the liquor into a tub to cool; when all but cold add a little yeast spread upon a slice of toasted bread; let it stand in a warm room. When fermentation is set up, put the mixture into a cask, and fill up from time to time as the yeast runs out of the bunghole; when the fermentation is finished, bung it down, leaving a peg-hole which can afterwards be closed, and in less than a year it will be fit to bottle.

Stomach Bitters, equal to Hostetter's, for one-fourth its cost.—European Gentian root 1½ ounces; orange peel, 2½ ounces; cinnamon, ¼ ounce; anise seed, ½ ounce; coriander seed, ½ ounce; cardamon seed, ⅛ ounce; unground Peruvian bark, ½ ounce; gum kino, ¼ ounce; bruise all these articles, and put them into the best alcohol, 1 pint; let it stand a week and pour off the clear tincture; then boil the dregs a few minutes in 1 quart of water, strain, and press out all the strength; now dissolve loaf sugar, 1 pound, in the hot liquid, adding 3 quarts cold water, and mix with spirit tincture first poured off, or you can add these, and let it stand on the dregs if preferred.

Soda Syrup, with or without Fountains.—The common or more watery syrups are made by using loaf or crushed sugar, 8 pounds; pure water, 1 gallon; gum arabic, 2 ounces; mix in a brass or copper kettle; boil until the gum is dissolved, them skim and strain through white flannel, after which add tartaric acid, 5½ oz. dissolved in hot water; to flavor use extract of lemon, orange rose, pine-apple, peach, sarsaparilla, strawberry, &c., ½ ounce to each bottle, or to your taste.

Bead for Liquor.—The best bead is the orange-flower water bead, (oil of neroil,) 1 drop in each gallon of brandy. *Another method:*—To every 40 drops of sulphuric acid, add 60 drops purest sweet oil in a glass vessel|; use immediately. This quantity is generally sufficient for 10 gallons spirit. *Another.*—Take 1 ounce of the purest oil sweet almonds; 1 ounce of sulphuric acid; put them in a stone mortar, add by *degrees*, 2 ounces white lump sugar, rubbing it well with the pestle till it becomes a paste; then add small quantities of spirits of wine till it comes into a liquid; This quantity is sufficient for 100 gallons. The first is strongly recommended as the best.

Coloring for Liquors.—Take 2 pounds crushed or lump sugar, put it into a kettle that will hold 4 to 6 quarts, with ½ tumbler of water. Boil it until it is *black*, then take it off and cool with water, stirring it as you put in the water.

Wax Putty for Leaky Cans, Bungs, etc.—Spirits turpentine, 2 lbs.; tallow, 4 pounds; solid turpentine, 12 pounds. Melt the wax and solid turpentine together over a slow fire, then add the tallow. When melted, remove far from the fire, then stir the spirits turpentine, and let it cool.

Cement for the Mouths of Corked Bottles.—Melt together ¼ of a pound of rosin, a couple of ounces of beeswax. When it froths stir it with a tallow candle. As soon as it melts, dip the mouths of the corked bottles into it. This is an excellent thing to exclude the air from such things as are injured by beitg exposed to it.

DRUGGISTS' DEPARTMENT.

Arnica Liniment.—Add to one pint of sweet oil, two tablespoonfuls of tincture of arnica; or the leaves may be heated in the oil over a slow fire. Good for wounds, stiff joints, rheumatic, and all injuries.

Ayer's Cherry Pectoral.—Take four grains of acetate of morphia, 2 fluid drachms of tincture of bloodroot, 7 fluid drachms each of antimonial wine and wine of ipecacuanha and three fluid ounces of syrup of wild cherry. Mix.

Balm Gilead.—Balm-gilead buds, bottled up in new rum, are very healing to fresh cuts or wounds. No family should be without a bottle,

Blackberry Cordial.—To one quart of blackberry juice, add one pound of white sugar, one tablespoonful of cloves, one of allspice, one of cinnamon, and one of nutmeg. Boil all together fifteen minutes; add a wineglass of whiskey, brandy, or rum. Bottle while hot, cork tight, and seal. This is a specific in diarrhœa. One dose, which is a wineglassful for an adult—half that quantity for a child—will often cure diarrhœa. It can be taken three or four times a day if the case is severe.

Brandreth's Pills.—Take two pounds of aloes, one pound of gamboge, four ounces of extract of colocynth, half a pound of castile soap, two fluid drachms of oil of peppermint; and one fluid drachm of cinnamon. Mix and form into pills.

Brown's Bronchial Troches.—Take one pound of pulverized extract of licorice, one and a half pounds of pulverized sugar, four ounces of pulverized cubebs, four ounces of pulverized gum arabic, and one ounce of pulverized extract of conium. Mix.

Bryan's Pulmonic Wafers, for Coughs, Colds, &c.—Take white sugar, 7 pounds; tincture of syrup of ipecac, four ounces; antimonial wine, two ounces; morphine, ten grains; dissolved in a tablespoonful of water, with ten or fifteen drops sulphuric acid; tincture of bloodroot; one ounce; syrop of tolu, two ounces; add these to the sugar, and mix the whole mass as confectioners do for lozenges, and cut into lozenges the ordinary size. Use from six to twelve of these in twenty-four hours. They sell at a great profit.

Candied Lemon or Peppermint, for Colds.—Boil one and a half pounds of sugar in a half pint of water, till it begins to candy round the sides; put in eight drops of essence; pour it upon buttered paper, and cut it with a knife.

Camphor Balls, for rubbing on the hands to prevent chaps, &c. Melt three drachms of spermaceti, four drachms of white wax, and one ounce of almond oil; stir in three drachms of powdered camphor. Pour the compound into small gillipots, so as to form small hemispherical cakes. They may be colored with alkanet, if preferred.

Camphorated Oil.—This is another camphor liniment, The proportions are the same as in the preceding formula, substituting olive oil for the alcohol, and exposing the materials to a moderate heat. As an external stimulant application it is even more powerful than the spirits; and to obtain its full influence the part treated should be also covered with flannel and oil silk. It forms a valuable liniment in chronic rheumatism and other painful affections, and is specially valuable as a counter-irritant in sore or inflamed throats and diseased bowels. Camphor constitutes the basis of a large number of valuable liniments. Thus, in cases of whooping-cough and some chronic bronchitic affections, the following liniment may be advantageously rubbed into the chest and along the spine. Spirits of camphor, two parts; laudanum, half a part; spirits of turpentine, one part; castile soap in powder, finely divided, half an ounce; alcohol, 3 parts. Digest the whole together for three days, and strain through linen. This liniment should be gently warmed before using. A powerful liniment for old rheumatic pains, especially when affecting the loins, is the following: camphorated oil and spirits of turpentine, of each two parts; water of hartshorn, one part; laudanum, one part; to be well shaken together. Another efficient liniment or embrocation, serviceable in chronic painful affections, may be conveniently and easily made as follows: Take of camphor, one ounce; cayenne pepper, in powder, two teaspoonfuls; alcohol, one pint. The whole to be digested with moderate heat for ten days, and filtered. It is an active rubificant; and after a slight friction with it, it produces a grateful thrilling sensation of heat in the pained part, which is rapidly relieved.

Camphor Tablet for Chapped Hands, &c.—Melt tallow, and add a little powdered camphor and glycerine, with a few drops of oil of almonds to scent. Pour in moulds and cool.

Camphorated Eye-Water.—Sulphate of copper, 15 grains; French bole, 15 grains; camphor, 4 grains; boiling water, 4 oz. Infuse, strain, and dilute with 2 quarts of cold water.

Canker Cure.—Take one large teaspoonful of water, two teaspoonfuls of honey, two of loaf sugar, three of powdered sage, two of powdered gold-thread, and one of alum. Stir up all together; put into a vessel, and let it simmer moderately over a steady fire. An oven is better. Then bottle for use. Give a teaspoonful occasionally through the day.

Cephalic Snuff.—Dried asarbacca leaves, three parts; marjoram, one part; lavender flowers, one part; rub together to a powder.

Certain Cure for Eruptions, Pimples, &c.—Having in numberless instances seen the good effects of the following precription, I can certify to its perfect remedy: Dilute corrosive sublimate with the oil of almonds, apply it to the face occasionally, and in a few days a cure will be effected.

Certain Cure for Headache and all Neuralgic Pains.—Opodeldoc, spirits of wine, sal ammoniac, equal parts. To be applied as any other lotion.

Chamomile Pills.—Aloes, 12 grains; extract chamomile, 36 grains; oil of chamomile, 3 drops; make into twelve pills; two every night, or twice a day.

Chlorine Pastiles for Disinfecting the Breath.—Dry chloride of lime, 2 drachms; sugar, 8 ounces; starch, 1 ounce: gum tragacanth, 1 drachm; carmine, 2 grains. Form into small lozenges.

2. Sugar flavored with vanilla, 1 ounce; powdered tragacanth, 20 grains; liquid chloride of soda sufficient to mix; add 2 drops of any essential oil. Form a paste and divide into lozenges of 15 grains each.

Cholera Morbus.—Take two ounces of the leaves of the bene-plant, put them in half a pint of cold water, and let them soak an hour. Give two tablespoonfuls hourly, until relief is experienced.

Cholera Remedy.—Spirits of wine, one ounce; spirits of lavender, quarter ounce; spirits of camphor, quarter ounce; compound tincture of benzion, half an ounce; oil of origanum, quarter ounce; twenty drops of moist sugar. To be rubbed outwardly also.

2. Twenty-five *minims* of diluted sulphuric acid in an ounce of water.

Corn Remedy.—Soak a piece of copper in strong vinegar for twelve or twenty-four hours. Pour the liquid off, and bottle. Apply frequently, till the corn is removed.

2. Supercarbonate of soda, one ounce, finely pulverized, and mixed with half an ounce of lard. Apply on a linen rag every night.

Cough Compound.—For the cure of coughs, colds, asthma, whooping cough, and all diseases of the lungs: One spoonful of common tar, three spoonfuls of honey, the yolk of three hen's eggs, and half a pint of wine; beat the tar, eggs and honey well together with a knife, and bottle for use. A teaspoonful every morning, noon, and night, before eating.

Cough Lozenges.—Powdered lactucarium, two drachms; extract of licorice root, twelve drachms; powdered squills, fifteen grains; refined sugar, six ounces; mucilage of tragacanth sufficient to mix. Make into two hundred and forty equal lozenges.

Cough Mixture.—Four drachms paregoric, with two drachms of sulphuric ether, and two drachms tincture of tolu. Dose, a teaspoonful in warm water.

Cough Syrup.—Put one quart hoarhound to one quart water, and boil it down to a pint; add two or three sticks of licorice and a tablespoonful of essence of lemon. take a tablespoonful of the syrup three times a day, or as often as the cough may be troublesome. The above recipe has been sold for $100. Several firms are making much money by its manufacture.

Cure for Diarrhœa.—The following is said to be an excellent cure for the above distressing complaint: Laudanum, two ounces; spirits of camphor, two ounces; essence of peppermint, two ounces; Hoffman's anodyne, two ounces; tincture of cayenne pepper, two drachms; tincture of ginger, one ounce. Mix all together. Dose, a teaspoonful in a little water, or a half teaspoonful repeated in an hour afterward in a tablespoonful of brandy. This preparation, it is said, will check diarrhœa in ten minutes, and abate other premonitory symptoms of cholera immediately. In cases of cholera, in has been used with great success to restore reaction by outward application.

Digestive Pills.—Rhubarb, 2 ounces; ipecacuanha, ½ ounce; cayenne pepper, ¼ ounce; soap, ½ ounce; ginger, ¼ ounce; gamboge, ½ ounce. Mix, and divide into four grain pills.

Dinner Pills.—Aloes, twenty grains; ginger, half a drachm; add syrup sufficient to mix. Divide into twenty pills. One to be taken daily, before dinner.

Disease of the Bowels.—Take equal parts of syrup of rhubarb, paregoric, and spirits of camphor, mix together. For an adult, one teaspoonful. If necessary, it may be repeated in 2 or 3 hours.

Dried Herbs.—All herbs which are to be dried should be washed, separated, and carefully picked over, then spread on a coarse paper and keep in a room until perfectly dry. Those which are intended for cooking should be stripped from the stems and rubbed very fine. Then put them in bottles and cork tightly. Put those which are intended for medicinal purposes into paper bags, and keep them in a dry place.

Dysentery.—In diseases of this kind, the Indians use the roots and leaves of the blackberry bush—a decoction of which in hot water, well boiled down, is taken in doses of a gill before each meal, and before retiring to bed. It is an almost infallible cure.

Dysentery Specific, (particularly for bloody dysentery in Adults and Children.)—Take one pound gum arabic, one ounce gum tragacanth, dissolved in two quarts of soft water, and strained. Then take one pound of cloves, half a pound of cinnamon, half a pound allspice, and boil in two quarts of soft water, and strain. Add it to the gums, and boil all together over a moderate fire, and stir into it two pounds of loaf sugar. Strain the whole again when you take it off, and when it is cool, add to it half a pint sweet tincture of rhubarb, and a pint and a half of best brandy. Cork it tight in bottles, as the gums will sour, if exposed. If corked properly it will keep for years.

Anti-Bilious Pills.—Compound extract of colocynth, 60 grains; rhubarb, 30 grains; soap, 10 grains. Make into 24 pills. Dose, 2 to 4.

2. Compound extract of colocynth. 2 drachms; extract of rhubarb, half a drachm; soap, 10 grains. Mix, and divide into 40 pills. Dose, 1, 2, or 3.

3. Scammony, 10 to 15 grains; compound extract of colocynth, 2 scruples; extract of rhubarb, half a drachm; soap, 10 grains; oil of caraway, 5 drops. Make into 20 pills. Dose, 1 or 2, as required.

Great Pain Extractor.—Spirits of ammonia, one ounce, laudanum, one ounce; oil of organum, one ounce; mutton tallow, half-pound; combine the articles with the tallow when it is nearly cool.

Godfrey's Cordial.—Sassafras, six ounces; seeds of coriander, caraway, and anise, of each one ounce; infuse in six pints of water; simmer the mixture till reduced to four pints; then add six pounds of molasses; boil a few minutes; when cold, add three fluid ounces of tincture of opium. For children teething.

Hooper's Female Pills.—Sulphate of iron, eight ounces; water, eight ounces; dissolve, and add Barbadoes aloes, forty ounces; myrrh, two ounces; make twenty pills. Dose, 2 to 6.

Hydrophobia—to Prevent.—Elecampane, one drachm; chalk, four drachms; Armenian bole, three drachms; alum, ten grains; oil of anise-seed, five drops.

Infant's Syrup.—The syrup is made thus: one pound best box raisins, half an ounce of anise-seed, two sticks licorice; split the raisins, pound the anise-seed, and cut the licorice fine; add to it three quarts of rain water, and boil down to two quarts. Feed three or four times a day, as much as the child will willingly drink. The raisins are to strengthen, the anise is to expel the wind, and the lorice as a physic.

Basilicon Ointment.—Good resin, five parts; lard, eight parts; yellow wax, two parts. Melt, and stir together till cool.

Cancer Ointment.—White arsenic, sulphur, powdered flowers of lesser spearwort, and stinking chamomile, levigated together and formed into a paste with white of egg.

Elder Flower Ointment.—Lard, twenty-five pounds; prepared mutton suet, five pounds; melt in an earthen vessel; add elder flower water, three gallons. Agitate for half an hour, and set it aside: the next day gently pour off the water, remelt the ointment, add benzoic acid three drachms; otto of roses, twenty drops; essence of bergamot and oil of rosemary, of each, thirty drops; again agitate well, let it settle for a few minutes, and pour off the clear into pots.

Eruption Ointment, for Frosted Feet, &c.—Chrome yellow and hog's lard.

Foot Ointment. (for all domestic animals.)—Equal parts of tar, lard and resin, melted together.

Golden Ointment.—Orpiment, mixed with lard to the consistence of an ointment.

Pile Ointment.—Powdered nutgall, two drachms; camphor, one drachm; melted wax, one ounce; tincture of opium, two drachms. Mix.

Ointment.—Take equal parts of yellow root or gold thread and common elder bark, and simmer them in hog's lard. No family should be without this ointment. It is good for chapped hands, chilblains, burns, scalds, sore nipples and lips.

Swaim's Vermifuge.—Wormseed, two ounces; valerian, rhubarb, pink-root, white agaric, of each, one and a half ounces;

boil in sufficient water to yield three quarts of decoction, and add it to thirty drops of oil of tansy, and forty-five drops of oil of cloves, dissolved in a quart of rectified spirits. Dose, one teaspoonful at night.

For Tetter, Ringworm and Scald Head.—One pound simple cerate; sulphuric acid, one quarter pound; mix together, and ready for use.

Tincture for Wounds.—Digest flowers of St. Johnswart, one handful, in half a pint of rectified spirits, then express the liquor and dissolve in it myrrh, aloes and dragon's blood, of each one drachm, with Canada balsam, half an ounce.

Tonic.—The following is the tonic used by reformed drunkards to restore the vigor of the stomach. Take of gentian root, half an ounce; valerian root, one drachm; best rhubarb root, two drachms; bitter orange peel, three drachms; cardamon seeds, half an ounce, and cinnamon bark, one drachm. Having bruised all the above together in a mortar (the druggist will do it if requested), pour upon it one and a half pints of boiling water and cover up close; let it stand till cold; strain, bottle and cork securely; keep in a dark place. Two tablespoonfuls may be taken every hour before meals, and half that quantity whenever the patient feels that distressing sickness and prostration so generally present for some time after alcoholic stimulants have been abandoned.

Whooping Cough.—Mix a quarter of a pound of ground elcampane root in half a pint of strained honey and half a pint of water. Put them in a glazed earthen pot, and place it in a stone oven, with half the heat required to bake bread. Let it bake until about the consistency of strained honey, and take it out. Administer in doses of a teaspooful before each meal, to a child; if an adult, double the dose.

Wild Cherry Bitters.—Boil a pound of wild cherry bark in a quart of water till reduced to a pint. Sweeten and add a little rum to preserve, or, if to be used immediately, omit the rum. Dose, a wineglassful three times a day, on an empty stomach.

A Certain Cure for Drunkenness,—Sulphate of iron, 5 grains; magnesia, 10 grains; peppermint water, 11 drachms; spirits of nutmeg, 1 drachm; twice a day. This preparation acts as a tonic and stimulant, and so partially supplies the place of the accustomed liquor, and prevents that absolute physical and moral prostration that follows that sudden breaking off from the use of stimulating drinks.

MANUFACTURERS' DEPARTMENT.

Indelible Ink for Marking Clothing.—Nitrate of silver, 5 scruples; gum arabic, 2 drachms; sap green, 1 scruple; distilled water, 1 ounce; mix together. Before writing on the article to be marked; apply a little of the following; carbonate of soda, one-half ounce, distilled water, four ounces; let this last, which is the mordant, get dry; then with a quill pen, write what you require.

Imitation Gold.—16 parts platina; 7 parts copper; 1 part zinc, put in a covered crucible, with powdered charcoal, and melt together till the whole forms one mass and are thoroughly incorporated together. Or take 4 oz. platina, 3 oz. silver, 1 oz. copper.

Imitation Silver.—11 oz. refined nickel; 2 oz. metalic bismuth. Melt the compositions together three times, and pour them out in lye. The third time, when melting, add 2 oz. pure silver. Or take ¼ oz. copper; 1 oz. bismuth; 2 oz. saltpeter; 2 oz. common salt, 1 oz. arsenic; 1 oz. potash; 2 oz. brass, and 3 oz. pure silver. Melt all together in a crucible.

Recipe for Making Artificial Honey.—To 10 pounds sugar add 3 pounds water; 40 grains cream tartar; 10 drops essence peppermint; and 3 pounds strained honey. First dissolve the sugar in water and take off the scum; then dissolve the cream of tartar in a little warm water which you will add with some little stirring; then add the honey; heat to a boiling point, and stir for a few minutes.

Vinegar.—Take forty gallons of soft water, six quarts of cheap molasses, and six pounds of acetic acid; put them into a barrel (an old vinegar barrel is best), and let them stand from three to ten weeks, stirring occasionally. Add a little "mother" of old vinegar if convenient. Age improves it.

Soft Soap.—Dissolve fifteen pounds of common cheap hard soap in fifteen gallons of hot water, and let it cool. Then dissolve fifteen pounds of sal soda in fifteen gallons of hot water; add six pounds of unslaked lime, and boil twenty minutes. Let it cool and settle, and then pour off the clear liquor very carefully and mix it with the soap solution. It improves it very much to add one quart of alcohol after mixing the two solutions. Smaller quantities can be made in the same proportions. If too strong, add water to suit.

Babbit's Premium Soap,—5 gallons strong lye; 5 gallons water; 5 lbs. tallow; 1 lb. potash; 2 lbs. sal soda; ½ lb. rosin; 1 pint salt; 1 pint washing fluid. Let the water boil; then put in the articles, and boil half an hour. Stir it well while boiling, and then run into moulds. It will be ready for use as soon as cold. The above preparations are for 100 pounds of soap.

Imitation of the Ruby.—Strass, eight parts; oxide of manganese, two parts; mix and fuse same as topaz.

Imitation Emerald.—Strass, five hundred parts; glass of antimony, twenty parts; oxide of cobalt, three parts; fuse with care for twenty-four hours, then cool slowly.

Imitation Sapphire.—Oxide of cobalt, one part; strass, eight parts. Fuse carefully for thirty-six hours.

Paste Resembling the Diamond.—Take white sand, nine hundred parts; red lead, six hundred parts; pearl-ash four hundred and fifty parts; nitre, three hundred parts; arsenic, fifty parts; manganese, half a part. To make it harder, use less lead, and if it should have a yellow tint, add a little more manganese.

Imitation Topaz.—Strass, five hundred parts; glass of antimony, twenty-one parts; purple of cassius, half a part; fuse for twenty-fore hours, and cool slowly.

Celebrated Recipe for Silver Wash.—One ounce of nitric acid, one ten-cent piece, and one ounce of quick silver. Put in an open glass vessel, and let it stand until dissolved; then add one pint of water, and it is ready for use. Make it into a powder by adding whiting, and it may be used on brass, copper, German silver, ect.

Cement for Aquaria.—Many persons have attempted to make aquariums, but have failed on account of the extreme difficulty in making the tank resist the action of water for any length of time. Below is a recipe for a cement that can be relied upon; it is perfectly free from anything that injures the animals or plants; it sticks to glass, metal, wood, stone, etc., and hardens under water. A hundred different experiments with cement have been tried, but there is nothing like it. It is the same as that used in constructing the tanks used in the Zoological Gardens, London, and is almost unknown in this country. One part, by measure, say a gill, of litharge; one gill of plaster of Paris; one gill of dry, white sand; one-third of a gill of finely-powdered resin. Sift and keep corked tight until required for use, when it is to be made into a putty by mixing in boiled oil (linseed) with a little patent dryer added. Never use it after it has been mixed (that is, with the oil) over fifteen hours. This cement can be used for marine as well as fresh water aquaria, as it resists the action of salt water. The tank can be used immediately, but it is best to give it three or four hours to dry.

Cement for Attaching Metal to Glass.—Take two ounces of a thick solution of glue, and mix it with one ounce of linseed-oil varnish, and half an ounce of pure turpentine; the whole are then boiled together in a close vessel. The two bodies should be clamped and held together for about two days after they are united, to allow the cement to become dry. The clamps may then be removed.

Cement for Mending Broken China.—Stir plaster of Paris into a thick solution of gum arabic, till it becomes a viscous paste. Apply it with a brush to the fractured edges, and draw the parts closely together.

Cement for Mending Steam Boilers.—Mix two parts of finely powdered litharge with one part of very fine sand, and one part of quicklime which has been allowed to slack spontaneously by exposure to the air. This mixture may be kept for any length of time without injury. In using it a portion is mixed into paste with linseed oil, or, still better, boiled linseed oil. In this state it must be quickly applied, as it soon becomes hard.

Cheap Galvanic Battery.—Take a cylindrical vessel, and put another of porous porcelain inside of it; fill the vessel with diluted sulphuric acid, and the space between the two with sulphate of copper (if you require to plate the article with copper); if not, a solution of the salt of gold, silver, etc., according to that which you wish it to be; put a slip of zinc in the sulphuric acid, and attach a copper wire to it, and the other end to the metal or other article you wish to plate, and immerse that in the other solution. Your battery is now complete. If you want the copper to be very thick, you must put a few solid crystals of copper in the solution; where you do not want it to come in contact, you must touch it with a little grease; if you want to take the copper off the article, you must do it over with a slight varnish.

Cheap White House Paint.—Take skim milk, two quarts, eight ounces fresh slaked lime, six ounces linseed oil, two ounces white Burgundy pitch, three pounds spanish white. Slake the lime in water, expose it to the air, and mix in about one-quarter of the milk; the oil, in which the pitch is previously dissolved to be added, a little at a time; then the rest of the milk, and afterwards the Spanish white. This quantity is sufficient for thirty square yards, two coats, and costs but a few cents. If the other colors are wanted, use, instead of Spanish white, other coloring matter.

Composition for House-Roofs.—Take one measure of fine sand, two of sifted wood-ashes, and three of lime, ground up with oil. Mix thoroughly, and lay on with a painter's brush, first a thin coat and then a thick one. This composition is not only cheap, but it strongly resists fire.

Diamond Cement.—Isinglass, one ounce; distilled vinegar, five and a half ounces; spirits of wine, two ounces; gum ammoniacum, half an ounce, gum mastic, half an ounce. Mix well.

French Polish.—To one pint of spirits of wine, add a quarter of an ounce of gum copal, quarter of an ounce of gum arabic, and one ounce of shellac. Let the gums be well bruised, and sifted through a piece of muslin. Put the spirits and the gums together in a vessel that can be closely corked; place them near a warm stove, and frequently shake them; in two or three days they will be dissolved; strain the mixture through a piece of muslin, and keep it tightly corked for use.

Furniture Oil for Polishing and Straining Mahogany.—Take of linseed oil, one gallon; alkanet root, three ounces; rose pink, one ounce. Boil them together ten minutes, and strain so that the oil will be quite clear. The furniture should be well rubbed with it every day until the polish is brought up, which will be more durable than any other.

Furniture Polish.—Take equal parts of sweet oil and vinegar, mix. add a pint of gum arabic, finely powdered. This will make furniture look almost as good as new, and can be easily applied, as it requires no rubbing. The bottle should be shaken, and the polish poured on a rag and applied to the furniture.

Glue for ready Use.—To any quantity of glue use common whiskey instead of water. Put both together in a bottle, cork tight, and set it away for three or four days, when it will be fit for use without the application of heat.

A Quart of Ink for a Dime.—Buy extract of logwood, which may be had at three cents an ounce, or cheaper by the quantity. Buy also, for three cents, an ounce of *bi-chromate of potash.* Do not make a mistake, and get the simple chromate of potash. The former is orange red, and the latter clear yellow. Now, take half an ounce of extract of logwood and ten grains of bi-chromate of potash, and dissolve them in a quart of hot rain water. When cold, pour it into a glass bottle, and leave it uncorked for a week or two. Exposure to the air is indispensable. The ink is then made, and has cost five to ten minutes' labor, and about three cents, besides the bottle. The ink is at first an intense steel blue, but becomes quite black.

An Excellent Substitute for Ink.—Put a couple of iron nails into a teaspoonful of vinegar. In half an hour pour in a tablespoonful of strong tea, and then you will have ink enough for a while.

Ink, First-Rate Black.—Take twelve pounds of bruised galls, five pounds of gum Senegal, five pounds of green sulphate of iron, and twelve gallons of rain water. Boil the galls with nine gallons of water for three hours, adding fresh water to replace what is lost by evaporation. Let the decoction settle, and draw off the clear liquor; add to it a strained solution of the gum; dissolve also the sulphate of iron separately, and mix the whole.

Another.—Galls, three pounds; sulphate of iron, one pound; logwood, half a pound; gum half a pound; ale, four gallons. Let it stand in loosely corked bottles in a warm place for a week or two, shaking it daily.

Ink, Blue.—Chinese blue, three ounces; oxalic acid, (pure,) three-quarters of an ounce; gum arabic, powdered, one ounce; distilled water, six pints. Mix.

Ink, Blue, Easily Made.—The soluble indigo of commerce makes a good blue ink when slightly diluted with hot water. It is incorrosive for steel pens, and flows freely.

Ink, Cheap Black.—Extract of logwood, two ounces; sulphate o f potash, quarter of an ounce; boiling water, one gallon. Mix. This is as excellent ink, and can be made at a cost not exceeding fifteen cents a gallon.

Ink, Cheap Printing.—Take equal parts of lampblack and oil; mix and keep on the fire till reduced to the right consistency. This is a good ink for common purposes and is very cheap. We have used it extensively ourselves.

Ink, Copying.—Dissolve half an ounce of gum and twenty grains of Spanish licorice in thirteen drachms of water, and add one drachm of lamp-black, previously mixed with a teaspoonful of sherry.

Another.—Common black ink, three parts; sugar candy, one part.

Ink, Indelible.—To four drachms of lunar caustic, in four ounces of water, add 60 drops of nutgalls, made strong by being pulverized and steeped in soft water. The mordant, which is to be applied to the cloth before writing, is composed of one ounce of pearlash, dissolved in four ounces of water, with a little gum arabic dissolved in it. Wet the spot with this; dry and iron the cloth; then write.

2. Nitrate of silver, five scruples; gum arabic, two drachms; sap green, one scruple; distilled water, one ounce. Mix together. Before writing on the article to be marked, apply a little of the following: carbonate of soda. half an ounce; distilled water, four ounces; let this last, which is the mordant, get dry; then with a quill, write what you require.

Ink, Indelible Marking.—One and a half drachms of nitrate of silver, one ounce of distilled water, half an ounce of strong mucilage of gum arabic, three-quarters of a drachm of liquid ammonia. Mix the above in a clean glass bottle, cork tightly, and keep in a dark place till dissolved, and ever afterwards. Directions for use; Shake the bottle, then dip a clean quill in the ink, and write or draw what you require on the article; immediately hold it close to the fire (without scorching,) or pass a hot iron over it, and it will become a deep and indelible black, indestructible by either time or acids, of any description.

Ink, Indestructible.—On many occasions it is of importance to employ an ink indestructable by any process, that will not equally destroy the material on which it is applied. For black ink, twenty-five grains of copal, in powder, are to be dissolved in two hundred grains of oil of lavender, by the assistance of a gentle heat, and are then to be mixed with two and a half grains of lamp-black and half a grain of indigo. This ink is particularly useful for labelling phials, etc., containing chemical substances of a corrosive nature.

Ink, for Marking Linen with Type.—Dissolve one part of asphaltum in four parts of oil of turpentine, and lamp-black or black-lead, in fine powder, in sufficient quantity to render of proper consistency to print with type.

Ink Powder for Immediate Use.—Reduce to powder ten ounces of gall-nuts, three ounces of green copperas, two ounces each of powdered alum and gum arabic put, |a little of this mixture into white wine, and it will be fit for immediate use.

Ink Stains.—The moment the ink is spilled, take a little milk, and saturate the stain, soak it up with a rag, and apply a little more milk, rubbing it well in. In a few minutes the ink will be completely removed.

Red Ink.—Take of the raspings of Brazil wood, quarter of a pound, and infuse them two or three days in colorless vinegar. Boil the infusion one hour and a half over a gentle fire, and afterward filter it while hot, through paper laid in an earthenware cullender. Put it again over the fire, and dissolve in it first half an ounce of gum arabic, and afterward of alum and white sugar each half an ounce. Care should be taken that the Brazil wood be not adulterated with the Braziletto or Campeachy wood.

Resin-oil Ink.—Melt together thirteen ounces of resin, one pound of resin-oil, and one and a half ounces of soft soap. When cold, add lamp-black.

Runge's Black Writing Fluid.—Boil twenty-two pounds of logwood in enough water to yield fourteen gallons of decoction. To each one thousand parts add one part of yellow chromate of potash. Stir the mixture.

Sympathetic Invisible Ink.—Sulphuric acid, one part; water, ten parts; mix together and write with a quill pen, which writing can be read only after heating it.

Sympathetic or Secret Inks.—Mix equal quantities of sulphate of copper and sal ammoniac, and dissolve in water. Writing done with this ink is invisible until the paper is heated, when it turns a yellow color. Lemon juice, milk, juice of onions, and some other liquids become black when the writing is held to the fire.

Transfer Ink.—Mastic in tears, four ounces; shellac, six ounces; Venice turpentine, half an ounce; melt together, add wax, half a pound; tallow, three ounces. When dissolved further add hard tallow soap (in shavings), three ounces; and when the whole is combined, add lamp-black two ounces. Mix well, cool a little, and then pour it into molds. This ink is rubbed down with a little water in a cup or saucer, in the same way as water color cakes. In winter, the operation should be performed near the fire.

Indian Glues,—Take one pound of the best glue, the stronger the beter, boil it and strain it very clear; boil also four ounces of isinglass; put the mixture into a double glue pot, add half a pound of brown sugar, and boil the whole until it gets thick; then pour it into thin plates or molds, and when cold you may cut and dry them in small pieces for the pocket. The glue is used by merely holding it over steam, or wetting it with the mouth. This is a most useful and convenient article, being much stronger than common glue. It is sold under the name of Indian glue, but is much less expensive in making, and is applicable to all kinds of small fractures, etc.; answers well on the hardest woods, and cements, china, etc., though, of course, it will not resist the action of hot water. For parchment and paper, in lieu of gum or paste, it will be found equally convenient.

Japanese Cement.—Intimately mix the best powdered rice with a little cold water, then gradually add boiling water until a proper consistence is acquired, being particularly careful to keep it well stirred all the time; lastly, it must be boiled for one minute in a clean saucepan or earthern pipkin. This glue is beautifully white and almost transparent, for which reason it is well adapted for fancy paper work, which requires a strong and colorless cement.

Liquid Blacking.—Mix a quarter of a pound of ivory-black, **six** gills of vinegar, a tablespoonful of sweet oil, and two large spoonfuls of molasses. Stir the whole well together, and it will then be fit for use.

Liquid Glue.—Dissolve one part of powdered alum, one hundred and twenty parts of water; add one hundred and twenty parts of glue, ten of acetic acid, and forty of alcohol, and digest. Prepared glue is made by dissolving common glue in warm water, and then adding acetic acid (strong vinegar) to keep it. Dissolve one pound of best glue in one and a half pints of water, and add one pint of vinegar. It is then ready for use.

Magic Copying Paper.—To make black paper, lamp-black mixed with cold lard; red paper, Venetian red mixed with lard; blue paper, Prussian blue mixed with lard; green paper, Chrome green mixed with lard. The above ingredients to be mixed to the consistency of thick paste, and to be applied to the paper with a rag. Then take a flannel rag, and rub until all color ceases coming off. Cut your sheets four inches wide and six inches long; put four sheets together, one of each color, and sell for twenty-five cents per package. The first cost will not exceed three cents.

Directions for writing with this paper: Lay down your paper upon which you wish to write; then lay on the copying paper, and over this lay any scrap of paper you chose; then take any hard pointed substance and write as you would with a pen.

Mahogany Stain.—Break two ounces of dragon's blood in pieces, and put them in a quart of rectified spirits of wine; let the bottle stand in a warm place, and shake it frequently. When dissolved, it is fit for use, and will render common wood an excellent imitation of mahogany.

Marine Glue.—Dissolve four parts of india-rubber in thirty-four parts of coal tar naphtha, aiding the solution with heat and agitation. The solution is then thick as cream, and it should be added to sixty-four parts of powdered shellac, which must be heated in the mixture till all is dissolved. While the mixture is hot it is poured on plates of metal, in sheets like leather. It can be kept in that state, and when it is required to be used, it is put into a pot and heated till it is soft, and then applied with a brush to the surfaces to be joined. Two pieces of wood joined with this cement can scarcely be sundered.

Parchment.—Paper parchment may be produced by immersing paper in a concentratic solution of choloride of zinc.

Silver Plating Fluid.—Dissolve one ounce of nitrate of silver in crystal, in twelve ounces of soft water; then dissolve in the water two ounces cyanuret of potash, shake the whole together, and let it stand till it becomes clear. Have ready some half ounce vials, and fill half full of Paris white, or fine whiting, and then fill up the bottles with the liquor and it is ready for use. The whiting does not increase the coating power—it only helps to clean the articles, and to save the silver fluid by half filling the bottle.

Amalgam of Gold.—Place one part of gold in a small iron saucepan or ladle, perfectly clean, then add eight parts of mercury, and apply a gentle heat, when the gold will dissolve; agitate the mixture for one minute, and pour it out on a clean plate or stone slab.

For gilding brass, copper, etc. The metal to be gilded is first rubbed over with a solution of nitrate of mercury, and then covered over with a thin film of the amalgam. On heat being applied the mercury volatilizes, leaving the gold behind.

A much less proportion of gold is often employed than the above, where a very thin and cheap gilding is required, as by increasing the quantity of the mercury, the precious metal may be extended over a much larger surface. A similar amalgam prepared with silver is used for silvering.

Amalgam for Mirrors,—Lead and tin, each one ounce; bismuth, two ounces; mercury, four ounces; melt as before, and add the mercury. These are used to silver mirrors, glass globes, etc., by warming the glass, melting the amalgam, and applying it.

Annealing Steel.—1. For a small quantity. Heat the steel to a cherry red in a charcoal fire, then bury in sawdust, in an iron box, covering the sawdust with ashes. Let stay until cold.— 2. For a larger quantity, and when it is required to be very "soft." Pack the steel with cast iron (lathe or plainer) chips in an iron box, as follows: Having at least ½ or ¾ inch in depth of chips in the bottom of box, put in a layer of steel, then more chips to fill spaces between the steel, and also the ½ or ¾ inch space between the sides of box and steel, then more steel; and lastly, at least 1 inch in depth of chips, well rammed down on top of steel.

Heat to and keep at a red heat for from two to four hours. Do not disturb the box until cold.

To make Bell Metal.—1. Melt together under powdered charcoal, 100 parts of pure copper, with 20 parts of tin, and unite the two metals by frequently stirring the mass. Product very fine.—2. Copper 3 parts; tin 1 part; as above. Some of the finest church bells in the world have this composition.—3. Copper 2 parts; tin 1 part; as above.—4. Copper 72 parts; tin 26½ parts; iron 1½ parts. The bells of small clocks or pendules are made of this alloy in Paris.

Brass to Make. 1. *Fine Brass.*—2 parts of copper to 1 part of zinc. This is nearly one equivalent each of copper and zinc, if the equivalent of the former metal be taken at 63-2; or 2 equivalents of copper to 1 equivalent of zinc, if it be taken with Liebig and Berzelius, at 31-6.

2. Copper 4 parts; zinc, 1 part. An excellent and very useful brass.

Cleansing Solution for Brass.—Put together two ounces sulphuric acid, an ounce and a half nitric acid, one drachm saltpetre and two ounces rain water. Let stand for a few hours, and apply by passing the article in and out quickly, and then washing off thoroughly with clean rain water. Old discolored brass chains treated in this way will look equally as well as when new. The usual method of drying is in sawdust.

To Cover Brass with beautiful Lustre Colors.—One ounce of cream of tartar is dissolved in one quart of hot water, to which is added half an ounce of tin salt (protochloride of tin) dissolved in four ounces of cold water. The whole is then heated to boiling, the clear solution decanted from a trifling precipitate, and poured under continual stirring into a solution of three ounces hyposulphite of soda in one-half a pint of water, whereupon it is again heated to boiling, and filtered from the separated sulphur. This solution produces on brass the various luster-colors, depending on the length of time during which the articles are allowed to stay in it. The colors at first will be light to dark gold yellow, passing through all the tints of red to an irridescent brown. A similar series of colors is produced by sulphide of copper and lead, which, however, are not remarkable for their stability; whether this defect will be obviated by the use of the tin solution, experience and time alone can show.

Bronzing Gun-Barrels.—The so-called butter of zinc used for bronzing gun-barrels is made by dissolving zinc in hydrochloric acid till no more free acid is left; which is secured by placing zinc in the acid until it ceases to be dissolved. The liquid is then evaporated until a drop taken out and placed on a piece of glass solidifies in cooling, when it is mixed with two parts of olive-oil for every three parts of the liquid. The barrels must be cleansed and warmed before applying the so-called butter, which put on with a piece of linen rag.

Bronzing Fluid.—For brown; Iron filings, or scales, 1 lb.; arsenic, 1 oz.. hydrochloric acid, 1 lb.; metallic zinc, 1 oz. The article to be bronzed is to be dipped in this solution till the desired effect is produced.

Bronze, Green.—Acetic acid, diluted, 4 pounds; green verditer, 2 ounces; muriate of ammonia, 1 ounce; common salt, 2 ounces; alum ½ ounce; French berries, ½ pound; boil them together till the berries have yielded their color, and strain. Olive bronze, for brass or copper.—Nitric acid, 1 ounce; hydrochloric acid, 2 ounces; titanium or palladium, as much as will dissolve, and add three pints of distilled water.

To Soften Cast-Iron, for Drilling.—Heat to a cherry red, having it lie level in the fire, then with a pair of cold tongs put on a piece of brimstone, a little less in size than you wish the hole to be when drilled, and it softens entirely through the piece; let it lie in the fire until a little cool, when it is ready to drill.

To Weld Cast-Iron.—Take of good clear white sand, three parts; refined solton, one part; fosterine, one part; rock salt, one part; mix all together. Take two pieces of cast-iron, heat them in a moderate charcoal-fire, occasionally taking them out while heating, and dipping them into the composition, until they are of a proper heat to weld, then at once lay them on the anvil, and gently hammer them together, and, if done carefully by one who understands welding iron, you will have them nicely welded together. One man prefers heating the metal, then cooling it in the water of common beans, and heat it again for welding.

Case-Hardening.—The operation of giving a surface of steel to pieces of iron, by which they are rendered capable of receiving great external hardness, while the interior portion retains all the toughness of good wrought iron. Iron tools, fire-irons, fenders, keys, etc., are usually case-hardened.

1. The goods, finished in every respect put polishing, are put into an iron box, and covered with animal or vegetable charcoal, and cemented at a red heat, for a period varying with the size and description of the articles operated on.

2. Cow's horn or hoof is to be baked or thoroughly dried, and pulverized. To this add an equal quantity of bay salt; mix them with stale chamber-lye, or white wine vinegar; cover the iron with this mixture, and bed it in the same in loam, or inclose it in an iron box; lay it then on the hearth of the forge to dry and harden; then put it into the fire, and blow till the lump has a blood-red heat, and no higher, lest the mixture be burnt too much. Take the iron out, and immerse it in water to harden.

3. The iron previously polished and finished, is to be heated to a bright red and rubbed or sprinkled over with prussiate of potash. As soon as the prussiate appears to be decomposed and dissipated, plunge the article into cold water.

4. Make a paste with a concentrated solution of prussiate of potash and loam, and coat the iron therewith; then expose it to a strong red heat, and when it has fallen to a dull red, plunge the whole into cold water.

To recut old Files and Rasps.—Dissolve 4 ounces of saleratus in 1 quart of water, and boil the files in it for half an hour; then remove, wash, and dry them. Now have ready, in a glass or stone ware vessel, 1 quart of rain water, into which you have slowly added 4 ounces of best sulphuric acid, and keep the proportions for any amount used. Immerse the files in this preparation for from six to twelve hours, according to fineness or coarseness of the file; then remove, wash them clean, dry quickly, and put a little sweet oil on them to cover the surface. If the files are coarse, they will need to remain in about twelve hours, but for fine files six to eight hours is sufficient. This plan is applicable to blacksmiths', gunsmiths', tinners', coppersmiths' and machinists' files. Copper and tin workers will only require a short time to take the articles out of their files, as the soft metals with which they become filled are soon dissolved. Blacksmiths' and saw-mill files require full time. Files may be re-cut three times by this process. The liquid may be used at different times if required. Keep away from children as it is poisonous.

Twist, Browning for Gun-Barrels.—Take spirits of nitre ¾ oz.; tincture of steel, ¾ oz.; (if the tincture of steel cannot be obtained, the unmedicated tincture of iron may be used, but it is not so good) black brimstone, ¼ oz.; blue vitriol ½ oz.; corrosive sublimate ¼ oz.; nitric acid, 1 dr. or 60 drops; copperas, ¼ oz.; mix with 1½ pints of rain water, keep corked, also, as the other, and the process of applying is also the same.

Gun Metal.—1. Melt together 112 pounds of Bristol brass, 14 pounds of spelter, and 7 pounds of block tin.—2. Melt together 9 parts of copper and 1 part of tin; the above compounds are those used in the manufacture of small and great brass guns, swivels, etc.

Chinese Method of Mending Holes in Iron.—The Chinese mend holes in cast-iron vessels as follows: They melt a small quantity of iron in a crucible the size of a thimble, and pour the molten metal on a piece of felt covered with wood-ashes. This is pressed inside the vessel against the hole, and as it exudes on the other side it is struck by a small roll of felt covered with ashes. The new iron then adheres to the old.

Common Pewter,—Melt in a crucible 7 pounds of tin, and when fused throw in 1 pound of lead, 6 oz. of copper and 2 oz. of zinc. This combination of metal will form an alloy of great durability and tenacity; also of considerable lustre.

Best Pewter.—The best sort of pewter consists of 100 parts of tin, and 17 of regulus of antimony.

Hard Pewter.—Melt together 12 pounds of tin, 1 pound of regulus of antimony, and 4 ounces of copper.

To Mend Broken Saws.—Pure silver 19 parts; pure copper 1 part; pure brass 2 parts; all are to be filed into powder and intimately mixed. Place the saw level upon the anvil, the broken edges in close contact, and hold them so; now put a small line of the mixture along the seam, covering it with a large bulk of powdered charcoal; now with a spirit lamp and a jeweler's blow-pipe, hold the cold-dust in place, and blow sufficient to melt the solder mixture; then with a hammer set the joint smooth, if not already so, and file away any superfluous solder; and you will be surprised at its strength.

Solder, to Adhere to Brass or Copper. — Prepare a soldering solution in this way : Pour a small quantity of muriatic acid on some zinc filings, so as to completely cover the zinc. Let it stand about an hour, and then pour off the acid, to which add twice its amount of water. By first wetting the brass or copper with this preparation, the solder will readily adhere.

Common Solder. — Put into a crucible 2 lbs. of lead, and when melted throw in 1 pound of tin. This alloy is that generally known by the name of solder. When heated by a hot iron and applied to tinned iron with powdered resin, it acts as a cement or solder.

Tempering Steel. — For tempering many kinds of tools, the steel is first hardened by heating it to a cherry red, and plunging it into cold water. Afterward the temper is drawn by moderately heating the steel again. Different degrees of hardness are required for different purposes, and the degree of heat for each of these, with the corresponding color, will be found in the annexed table.

Very pale straw color, 430° — the temper required for lancets.

A shade of darker yellow, 450° — for razors and surgical instruments.

Darker straw-yellow, 470° — for penknives.

Still darker yellow, 490° — chisels for cutting iron.

A brown yellow 500° — axes and plane-irons.

Yellow, slightly tinged with purple, °520 — table-knives and watch-springs.

Tempering Liquid. — 1. To 6 quarts soft water put in corrosive sublimate, 1 oz.; common salt, 2 handfuls ; when dissolved it is ready for use. The first gives toughness to the steel, while the latter gives the hardness. Be careful with this preparation, as it is a dangerous poison. — 2. Salt, ½ tea-cup; saltpetre, ½ oz.; alum, pulverized. 1 tea-spoon; soft water, 1 gallon ; never heat over a cherry red, nor draw any temper. — 3. Saltpetre, sal-ammoniac, and alum, of each 2 ounces; salt, 1½ pounds; water, 3 gallons and draw no temper. — 4. Saltpetre and alum, of each 2 ounces; sal-ammoniac, ½ ounce; salt, 1½ pounds; soft water, 2 gallons. Heat to a cherry red, and plunge in, drawing no temper.

Bayberry, or Myrtle Soap. — Dissolve two and a quarter pounds of white potash in five quarts of water, then mix it with ten lbs. of myrtle wax, or bayberry tallow. Boil the whole over a slow fire till it turns to soap, then add a teacup of cold water; let it boil ten minutes longer; at the end of that time turn it into tin molds or pans, and let them remain a week or ten days to dry; then turn them out of the molds. If you wish to have the soap scented, stir into it an essential oil that has an agreeable smell, just before you turn it into the molds. This kind of soap is excellent for shaving, and for chapped hands; it is also good for eruptions on the face. It will be fit for use in the course of three or four weeks after it is made, but it is better for being kept ten or twelve or months.

Chemical Soap, (for taking Oil, Grease, etc., from Cloth.)—Take five pounds of castile soap, cut fine; one pint alcohol; one pint soft water; two ounces aquafortis; one and a half ounces lampblack; two ounces of saltpetre; three ounces potash; one ounce of camphor; and four ounces of cinnamon, in powder. First dissolve the soap, potash and saltpetre, by boiling; then add all the other articles, and continue to stir until it cools; then pour into a box and let it stand twenty-four hours and cut into cakes.

Cold Soap.—Mix twenty-six pounds of melted and strained grease with four pailfuls of ley made of twenty pounds of white potash. Let the whole stand in the sun, stirring it frequently. In the course of the week, fill the barrel with weak ley.

Genuine Erasive Soap.—Two pounds of good castile soap; half a pound of carbonate of potash; dissolve in half a pint of hot water. Cut the soap in thin slices, and boil the soap with the potash until it is thick enough to mould in cakes; also add alcohol, half an ounce; camphor, half an ounce; hartshorn, half an ounce; color with half an ounce of pulverized charcoal.

Hard White Soap.—To fifteen pounds of lard or suet, made boiling hot, add slowly six gallons of hot lye, or solution of potash, that will bear up an egg high enough to leave a piece big as a shilling bare. Take out a little, and cool it. If no grease rise it is done. If any grease appears, add lye, and boil till no grease rises. Add three quarts of fine salt, and boil up again. If this does not harden well on cooling, add more salt. If it is to be perfumed, melt it next day, add the perfume, and run it in moulds or cut in cakes.

Labor-Saving Soap,—Take two pounds of sal-soda, two pounds of yellow bar soap, and ten quarts of water. Cut the soap in thin slices, and boil together for two hours; strain, and it will be fit for use. Put the clothes in soak the night before you wash, and to every pail of water in which you boil them, add a pound of soap. They will need no rubbing, merely rinse them out, and they will be perfectly clean and white.

To Make Good Soap.—To make matchless soap, take one gallon of soft soap, to which add a gill of common salt, and boil an hour. When cold, separate the lye from the crude. Add to the crude two pounds of sal soda, and boil in two gallons of soft water till dissolved. If you wish it better, slice two pounds of common bar soap and dissolve in the above. If the soft soap makes more than three pounds of crude, add in proportion to the sal soda and water.

To make Hard Soap from Soft.—Take seven pounds of good soft soap; four pounds sal soda; two ounces borax; one ounce hartshorn; half a pound of resin; to be dissolved in twenty-two quarts of water, and boiled about twenty minutes.

Whale Oil Soap. (for the destruction of insects.)—Render common lye caustic, by boiling it at full strength on quicklime; then take the lye and boil it with as much whale oil foot as it will saponify (change to soap), pour off into moulds, and, when cold, it is tolerably hard. Whale oil foot is the sediment produced in refining whale oil, and is worth two dollars per barrel.

Soluble Glass.—Mix ten parts of carbonate of potash, fifteen parts of powdered quartz, and one pound of charcoal. Fuse well together. The mass is soluble in four or five parts of boiling water, and the filtered solution, evaporated to dryness, yields a transparant glass, permanent in the air.

Tracing Paper.—In order to prepare a beautiful transparent, colorless paper, it is best to employ the varnish formed with Demarara resin in the following way: The sheets intended for this purpose are laid flat on each other, and the varnish spread over the uppermost sheet with a brush, until the paper appears perfectly colorless, without, however, the liquid thereon being visible. The first sheet is then removed, hung up for drying, and the second treated in the same manner. After being dried this paper is capable of being written on, either with chalk or pencil, or with steel pens. It preserves its colorless transparency without becoming yellow, as is frequently the case with that prepared in any other way.

Unsurpassable Blacking.—Put one gallon of vinegar into a stone jug, and one pound of ivory-black well pulverized, half a pound of loaf sugar, half an ounce of oil of vitriol, and seven ounces of sweet oil. Incorporate the whole by stirring.

2. Take twelve ounces each of ivory-black and molasses; spermaceti oil, four ounces; and white wine vinegar, two quarts. Mix thoroughly. This contains no vitriol, and therefore will not injure the leather. The trouble of making it is very little, and it would be well to prepare it for one's self, were it only to be assured that it is not injurious.

Varnish for Iron Work.—To make a good black varnish for iron work, take eight pounds of asphaltum and fuse it in an iron kettle; then add five gallons of boiled linseed oil, one pound of litharge, half a pound of sulphate of zinc (add these slowly, or it will fume over), and boil them for about three hours. Now add one and a half pounds of dark gum amber, and boil for two hours longer, or until the mass will become quite thick when cool, after which it should be thinned with turpentine to due consistency.

THE TOILET, PERFUMERY, Etc.

Hair Restorers and Invigorators.—There are hundreds; Lyon's, Wood's, Barry's, Bogle's, Jayne's, Storr's, Baker's Driscol's, Phalon's, Haskel's, Allen's, Spalding's, etc. But, though all under different names, are similar in principle, being vegetable oils dissolved in alcohol, with the addition of spirit of soap, and an astringent material, such as tincture of catechu; or infusion of bark. The best is to dissolve one ounce of castor oil in one quart of 95 alcohol, and add one ounce of tincture of cantharides, two ounces of tincture of catechu, two ounces of lemon juice, two ounces of tincture of cinchona; and to scent it, add oil of cinnamon, or oil of rosemary, or both.

To Cure Baldness.—Take water, one pint; pearl-ash, one-half ounce; onion juice, one gill. Mix, and cork in a bottle. Rub the head night and morning, with a rough towel, dipped in the mixture.

To Make the Hair Soft and Glossy.—Put one ounce of castor oil in one pint of bay rum or alcohol, and color it with a little of the tincture of alkanet root. Apply a little every morning.

Poudre Subtile for Removing Superfluous Hair.—Take powdered quick-lime, two parts; sulphuret of arsenic, one part; starch, one part; mix into a fine powder, and keep in a close corked bottle. When required for use, take a small quantity and add two or three drops of water, and apply on the part you desire to remove the hair from—let it remain about one minute, or until it becomes red, then wash off.

Chinese Depilatory for Removing Superfluous Hair.—Fresh burnt lime, sixteen ounces; pearl-ash, two ounces; sulphuret of potash, two ounces. Reduce them to fine powder in a mortar, then put it into closely corked phials. For use, the part must be first soaked in warm water, then a little of the powder made into a paste must be immediately applied. Should it irritate the skin, wash it off with hot water or vinegar.

Instantaneous Hair Dye.—Take one drachm of nitrate of silver, and add to it just sufficient rain water to dissolve it, *and no more;* then take strong spirits of ammonia, and gradually pour on the solution of silver; until it becomes as clear as water, (*the addition of the ammonia at first makes it brown;*) then wrap around the bottle two or three covers of blue paper, to exclude the light —otherwise it will spoil. Having made this obtain two drachms of gallic acid; put this into another bottle which will contain one-half pint; pour upon it hot water, and let it stand until cold —when it is fit for use.

Directions to Dye the Hair.—First wash the head, beard, or mustaches with soap and water; afterwards with clean water. Dry, and apply the gallic acid solution, with a clean brush. When it is almost dry, take a small tooth comb, and with a fine brush, put on the teeth of the comb a little of the silver solution, and comb it through the hair, when it will become a brilliant jet black. Wait a few hours; then wash the head again with clean water. If you want to make a brown dye, add double or treble the quantity of water to the silver solution, and you can obtain any shade of color you choose.

Whiskers or Mustache forced to Grow.—Cologne, two ounces; liquid hartshorn, one drachm; tincture cantharides, two drachms; oil rosemary, twelve drops; oil nutmeg, twelve drops, and lavender, twelve drops. This is the recipe used in making the celebrated GRAHAM ONGUENT.

To Make Hair Curl.—At any time you may make your hair curl the more easily by rubbing it with the beaten yolk of an egg washed off afterwards with clean water.

To Prevent Gray Hair.—When the hair begins to change color, the use of the following pomade has a beneficial effect in preventing the disease extending, and has the character of even restoring the color of the hair in many instances; Lard 4 ounces; spermaceti, 4 drachms; oxide of bismuth, 4 drachms. Melt the lard and spermaceti together, and when getting cold stir in the bismuth; to this can be added any kind of perfume, according to choice. It should be used whenever the hair requires dressing, It must not be imagined that any good effect speedily results; it is, in general, a long time taking place, the change being very gradual.

Liquid Rouge for the Complexion.—Four ounces of alcohol, two ounces of water, twenty grains of carmine; twenty grains of ammonia, six grains of oxalic acid, six grains of alum, mix.

Vinegar Rouge.—Cochineal, three drachms; carmine lake, three drachms; alcohol, six drachms; mix, and then put into one pint of vinegar, perfumed with lavender; let it stand a fortnight, then strain for use.

Pearl Powder for Complexion.—Take white bismuth, one pound; starch powder, one ounce; orris powder, one ounce. Mix and sift through lawn. Add a drop of ottar of roses or neroli.

Pearl Water for the Complexion.—Castile soap, one pound; water, one gallon. Dissolve, then add alcohol, one quart; oil of rosemary and oil of lavender, each two drachms. Mix well.

Complexion Pomatum.—Mutton grease, one pound; oxide of bismuth, four ounces; powdered French chalk, two ounces; mix.

Spanish Vermillion for the Toilette.—Take an alkine solution of bastard saffron, and precipitate the color with lemon juice; mix the precipitate with a sufficient quantity of finely powdered French chalk and lemon juice, then add a little perfume

Lily White. is nothing but purified chalk, scented.

To Remove Freckles and Tan.—Tincture of benzoin, one pint; tincture tolou, one-half pint; oil rosemary, one-half ounce. Put one teaspoonful of the above mixture in one-quarter pint of water, and with a towel wash the face night and morning.

Feuchtwanger's Tooth Paste.—Powdered myrrh, two ounces: burnt alum, one ounce; cream tartar, one ounce; cuttle fish bone, four ounces; drop lake, two ounces; honey, half a gallon; mix.

Fine Tooth Powder.—Powdered orris root, one ounce; peruvian bark, one ounce; prepared chalk, one ounce; myrrh, one-half ounce.

To Make Brown Teeth White.—Apply carefully over the teeth, a stick dipped in strong acetic or nitric acid, and immediately wash out the mouth with cold water. To make the teeth even, if irregular draw a piece of fine cord betwixt them.

Superior Cologne Water.—Alcohol, one gallon; add oil of cloves, lemon, nutmeg, and bergamot, each one drachm; oil neroli, three and a half drachms; seven drops of oil of rosemary, lavender and cassia; half a pint of spirits of nitre; half a pint of elder-flower water. Let it stand a day or two, then take a cullender and at the bottom lay a piece of white cloth, and fill it up, one-fourth of white sand, and filter through it.

Smelling Salts.—Super carbonate of ammonia, eight parts; put it in coarse powder in a bottle, and pour out lavender oil one part.

Bandoline for the Hair.—This mixture is best made a little at a time. Pour a tablespoonful of boiling water on a dozen quince seeds; and repeat when fresh is required.

Oil of Roses—For the Hair.—Olive oil, two pints; otto of roses, one drachm; oil of rosemary, one drachm, mix. It may be colored by steeping a little alkanet root in the oil (by heat) before scenting it.

Arnica Hair Wash.—When the hair is falling off and becoming thin, from the too frequent use of castor, Macassor oils, |&c., or when permature baldness arises from illness, the arnica hair wash will be found of great service in arresting the mischief. It is thus peepared: take elder water, half a pint; sherry wine, half a pint; tincture of arnica, half an ounce; alcoholic ammonia, one drachm—if this last named ingredient is old, and has lost its strength, then two drachms instead of one may be employed. The whole of these are to be mixed in a lotion bottle, and applied every night to the head with a sponge. Wash the head with warm water twice a week, Soft brushes only must be used during the growth of the young hair.

Ammonical Pomatum for Promoting the Growth of Hair.—Take almond oil, quarter of a pound; white wax, half an ounce; clarified lard, three ounces; liquid ammonia, a quarter fluid ounce; otto of lavender, and cloves, of each one drachm. Place the oil, wax, and lard, in a jar, which set in boiling water; when the wax is melted, allow the grease to cool till nearly ready to set, then stir in the ammonia and the perfume, and put into small jars for use. Never use a hard brush, nor comb the hair too much Apply the pomade at night only.

Artificial Bears' Grease.—Bear's grease is imitated by a mixture of prepared veal suet and beef marrow. It may be scented at pleasure. The following are some of the best compounds sold by that name.

1. Prepared suets, 3 ounces; lard, 1 ounce; olive oil, 1 ounce; oil of cloves 10 drops; compound tincture of benzoin, 1 drachm. Mix.

2. Lard, 1 pound; solution of carbonate of potash, 2 ounces. Mix.

3. Olive oil, 3 pints; white wax, 3 ounces; spermaceti, 1 ounce, scent with oil of roses and oil of bitter almonds.

Bears' Oil.—The best description of lard oil, properly perfumed, is far preferable to any other kind of oil.

Circassian Cream.—One pint of olive oil: three ounces white wax; two ounces spermaceti; half an ounce alkanet root. Digest the oil with the alkanet till sufficiently colored, strain, melt the wax and spermaceti with the oil, and, when sufficiently cool, add two and a half drachms oil of lavender, one drachm of essence and of ambergies.

Cosmetic Soap, for Washing the Hands.—Take a pound of castile soap, or any other nice old soap; scrape it fine; put it on the fire with a little water, stir it to a smooth paste; turn it into a bowl; or any kind of essence; beat it with a silver spoon till well mixed; thicken it with Indian meal, and keep it in small pots, closely covered; exposure to the air will harden it.

Cosmetic Wash for the Hair.—Red wine, one pound; salt, one drachm; sulphate of iron, two drachms; boil for a few minutes, add common verdigris, one drachm; leave it on the fire two minutes; withdraw it, and add two drachms of powdered nutgall. Rub the hair with the liquid, in a few minutes dry it with a warm cloth, and afterwards wash with water.

To Remove Dandruff.—Take a thimbleful of powdered refined borax, let it dissolve in a teacupful of water, first brush the head well, then wet a brush and apply it to the head. Do this every day for a week, and twice a week for a few times, and you will effectually remove the dandruff.

To make the Complexion Fair.—Take emulsion of bitter almonds, one pint; oxymuriate of quicksilver, two and a half grains; sal ammonia, one drachm. Use moderately for pimples, freckles, tanned complexions.

Eau de Cologne—Cologne Water.—Oil of lavender, oil of bergamot, oil of lemon, oil of neroli, each one ounce; oil of cinnamon, half an ounce; spirit of rosemary, fifteen ounces; highly rectified spirit, eight pints. Let them stand fourteen days; then distill in a water bath.

2. Essential oils of bergamot, lemon, neroli, orangepeel and rosemary, each twelve drops; cardamon seeds, one drachm; rectified spirits, one pint. It improves by age.

Eau de Rosieres.—Spirits of roses, 4 pints; spirits of jessamine, one pint; spirits of orange flowers, one pint; spirits of cucumber, two and a quarter pints; spirits of celery seed, two and a quarter pints; spirits of angelica root, two and three quarter pints; tincture of benzoin, three quarters of a pint; balsam of Mecca, a few drops.

Eau de Violettes.—Macerate five ounces of fine orris root in a quart of rectified spirits, for some days, and filter.

Esprit de Bouquet.—Oil af lavender, oil of cloves and oil of bergamot, each two drachms; otto of rose, and of oil of cinnamon, each, twenty drops; essence of musk, one drachm; rectified spirits one pint. Mix.

Essence of Ambergris.—Spirits of wine, half a pint; ambergris

24 grains. Let it stand for three days in a warm place, and filter.

Essence of Bergamot.—Spirits of wine, half a pint; bergamot peel, four ounces; as above.

Essence of Cedrat.—Essence of bergamot, one ounce; essence of neroli, two drachms.

Essence of Cloves.—Spirits of wine, half a pint; bruised cloves, one ounce.

Essence for the Headache.—Spirits of wine, two pounds; roche alum, in fine powder, two ounces; camphor, four ounces; essence of lemon, half an ounce; strong water of ammonia, four ounces. Stop the bottle close, and shake it daily, for three or four days.

Essence of Lavender. Essential oil of lavender, three and a half ounces; rectified spirits, two quarts; rose water, half a pint; tincture of orris, half a pint.

Essence of Lemon.—Spirits of wine, half a pint; fresh lemon peel, four ounces.

Essence of Musk.—Take one pint proof spirit, and add two drachms musk. Let it stand a fortnight, with frequent agitation.

Essence of Neroli.—Spirits of wine, half a pint; orange peel cut small, three onunces; orris root in powder, one drachm; musk, two grains.

Essence for Smelling Bottles.—Oil of lavender and essence of bergamot, each one drachm; oil of orange peel, eight drops; oil of cinnamon, four drops; oil of neroli, two drops; alcohol and strongest water of ammonia, each two ounces.

Essence of Verbena Leaf.—Take rectified spirits of wine, half a pint; otto of verbena, half a drachm; otto of bergamot one drachm; tincture of tolu, quarter of an ounce. Mix them together, and it is ready for use. This sweet scent does not stain the handkerchief and is very economical.

Essence of Violets.—Spirits of wine, half a pint; orris root, one ounce. Other essence in the same manner.

Eye Water,—Take one pint of rose water, and add one teaspponful each of spirits of camphor and laudanum. Mix and bottle. To be shaken and applied to the eyes as often as necessary. Perfectly harmless.

Honey Water.—Rectified spirits, eight pints; oil of cloves, oil of lavender, oil of bergamot, each half an ounce; musk, eight grains; yellow sandus shavings, four ounces; digest for eight days and add two pints each of orange flower and rose water.

Lavender Water.—Oil of lavender, four ounces; spirit, three quarts; rose water, one pint. Mix and filter.

Lisbon Water.—To rectified spirit, one gallon, add essential oils of orange peel and lemon peel, of each three ounces, and otto of roses, one quarter of an ounce.

Odoriferous Lavender Water.—Rectified spirit, five gallons; essential oil of lavender, twenty ounces; oil of bergamot, five ounces; essence of ambergris, half an ounce.

2. Oil of lavender, three drachms; oil of bergamot, twenty drops, nerolic, six drops; otto of roses, six drops; essence of cedrat, eight drops; essence of musk, twenty drops; rectified spirit, twenty-eight fluid ounces; distilled water, four ounces.

Queen of Hungary's Water.—Spirit of rosemary, four pints; orange flower water, one quarter of a pint; essence of neroli, four drops.

FACE PAINTS.

Almond Bloom.—Boil one ounce of Brazil dust in three pints of distilled water, and strain; add six drachms of isinglass, two drachms of cochineal, one ounce of alum, and eight drachms of borax; boil again and strain through a fine cloth.

Fine Carmine.—(prepared from cochineal) is used alone, or reduced with starch, etc. And also the coloring matter of safflower and other vegetable colors, in the form of pink saucers, &c.

Face Powder.—Starch, one pound; oxide of bismuth, four oz.

Face Whites.—French chalk is one of the most innocent; finely powdered. White starch is also used.

Rouge.—Mix vermillion with enough gum tragacanth dissolved in water to form a thin paste; add a few drops of almond oil, place the mixture in rough pots, and dry by a very gentle heat.

Turkish Rouge.—Take half pint alcohol and one ounce of alkanet; Macerate ten days and pour off the liquid, which should be bottled. This is the simplest and one of the best articles of the kind.

Caution.—White lead, and all cosmetic powders containing it should never be applied to the skin, as it is the most dangerous article that could be used.

Mouth Pastiles, for Perfuming the Breath.—Extract of licorice, three ounces; oil of cloves, one and a half drachms; oil of cinnamon fifteen drops. Mix, and divide into one-grain pills, and silver them.

2. Catechu, seven drachms; orris powder, forty grains; sugar, three ounces; oil of rosemary, (or of clove, peppermint, or cinnamon,) four drops. Mix, and roll flat on an oiled marble slab, and cut into very small lozenges.

Oil for the Hair.—A very excellent ready-made oil for the hair which answers all common purposes, is made by mixing one part brandy with three parts of sweet oil. Add any scent you prefer.

Oil of Roses.—Fine olive oil, one pint; otto of roses, sixteen drops. If required red, color with alkanet root, and strain before adding the otto. For common sale essence of bergamot or of lemon is often subtituted, wholly or in part, for the expensive otto.

Oil to make the Hair Curl—Olive, one pound; oil of origanum, one drachm; oil of rosemary, one and a quarter drachms.

HUNTERS AND TRAPPERS SECRETS.

The following secret applies to *all* animals, as every animal is attracted by the peculiar odor in a greater or less degree; but it is best adapted to land animals, such as Foxes, Minks, Sables, Martins, Wolves Bears, Wild Cats, etc., etc.

Take one half pound strained honey, one quarter drachm musk, three drachms oil of lavender, and four pounds of tallow, mix the whole thoroughly together, and make it into forty pills, or balls, and place one of these pills under the pan of each trap when setting it.

The above preparation will most wonderfully attract all kinds of animals, and trappers and others who use it will be sure of success.

To Catch Foxes.—Take oil of amber, and beaver's oil, each equal parts, and rub them over the trap before setting it. Set in the usual way.

To Catch Mink.—Take oil of amber, and beaver's oil, and rub over the trap. Bait with fish or birds.

To Catch Muskrat.—In the female muskrat near the vagina is a small bag which holds from 30 to 40 drops, Now all the trapper has to do, is to procure a few female muskrats and squeeze the contents of a bag into a vial. Now, when in quest of muskrats, sprinkle a few drops of liquid on the bushes over and around the trap. This will attract the male muskrats in large numbers, and if the traps are properly arranged, large numbers of them may be taken.

∗∗*In trapping Muskrats, steel traps should be used, and they should be set in the paths and runs of the animals, where they come upon the banks, and in every case the trap should be set under the water, and carefully concealed; and care should be taken that it has sufficient length of chain to enable the animals to reach the water after being caught, otherwise they are liable to escape by tearing or knawing of their legs.

To Catch Beaver.—In trapping for beaver, set the trap at the edge of the water or dam, at the point where the animals pass from deep to shoal water, and always beneath the surface, and fasten it by means of a stout chain to a picket driven in the bank, or to a bush or tree. A flat stick should be made fast to the trap by a cord a few feet long, which, if the animal chanced to carry away, the trap would float on the water and point out its position. The trap should then be baited with the following preparation, called

"*The Beaver Medicine.*"

This is prepared from a substance called castor, and is obtained from the glandulous pouches of the *male* animal.

The contents of five or six of these castor bags are mixed with a nutmeg, twelve or fifteen cloves and thirty grains of cinnamon in fine powder, and the whole thing well stirred together with as much whiskey as will give it the consistency of mixed mustard. This preparation must be left closely corked up, and in four or five days the odor becomes wonderful; and this medicine smeared upon the bits of wood etc., with which the traps are baited, will attract the beaver from a great distance, and wishing to make a close inspection, the animal puts its legs into the trap and is caught.

*₊*The same caution in regard to length of chain should be observed for Beaver, as for Otters, Muskrats, etc., for unless they can reach the water they are liable to get out of the trap and escape.

Chinese Art of Catching Fish.—Take Cocculus Indicus, pulverize and mix with dough, then scatter it broadcast over the water, as you would sow seed. The fish will sieze it with great avidity, and will instantly become so intoxicated that they will turn belly up on top of the water, by dozens, hundreds, or thousands, as the case may be. All that you now have to do, is to have a boat or other convenience to gather them up, and as you gather put them in a tub of clean water and presently they will be as lively and healthy as ever.

This means of taking fish, and the manner of doing it, has, heretofore, been known to but few. The value of such knowledge admits of no question. This manner of taking fish does not injure the flesh in the least.

Secret Art of Catching Fish.—Put the oil of rhodium on the bait, when fishing with the hook, and you will always succeed.

To Catch Fish.—Take the juice of smallage or lovage, and mix with any kind of bait. As long as there remain any kind of fish within many yards of your hook, you will find yourself busy pulling them out.

To Catch Abundance of Eels, Fish, &c.—Get over the water after dark, with a light and a dead fish that has been smeared with the juice of stinking glawdin—the fish will gather round you in large quantities, and can easily be scooped up.

THE FINE ARTS AND SCIENCES.

To Transfer Engravings to Plaster Casts.—Cover the plate with ink, polish its surface in the usual way, then put a wall of paper round; then pour on it some fine paste made with plaster of

Paris. Jerk it to drive out the air bubbles, and let it stand one hour, when you have a fine impression.

The New and Beautiful Art of Transferring on to Glass.—Colored or plain Engravings, Photographs, Lithographs, Water Colors, Oil Colors, Crayons, Steel Plates, Newspaper Cuts, Mezzotinto, Pencil, Writing, Show Cards, Labels,—or in fact anything.

Directions.—Take glass that is perfectly clear—window glass will answer—clean it thoroughly ; then varnish it, taking care to have it perfectly smooth ; place it where it will be entirely from dust; let it stand over night; then take your engraving, lay it in clear water until it is wet through (say ten or fifteen minutes) then lay it upon a newspaper, that the moisture may dry from the surface, and still keep the other side damp. Immediately varnish your glass the second time, then place your engraving on it, pressing it down firmly, so as to exclude every particle of air; next rub the paper from the back, until it is of uniform thickness—so thin that you can see through it, then varnish it the third time, and let it dry.

Materials used for the above Art.—Take two ounces balsam of fir, to one ounce of spirits of turpentine; apply with a camel's hair brush.

The Art of Potchiomoni.—Take plain glass jars or vases, in any shape, and clean them thoroughly ; then obtain two or three sheets of figures, flowers, or views, in imitation of Chinese, Egyptian, or Swiss painting. These goods, as well as the jars, can be obtained in any of the principal cities. Now, in whatever style you determine to ornament your vase or jar in, cut out the figures from your sheet, and secure them in different parts inside your jar, with the figures looking outwards. The best material for making them adhere is, to boil a piece of parchment; this makes a good size. Having secured the prints, make a varnish of balsam of fir and turpentine, and apply all over inside with a fine brush. When the first coat is dry, give another coat; now take any color you choose—black, blue, green, yellow, white; pink, brown or red—and grind the paint fine, with the best white varnish, and apply a coat of this paint over the whole inside; let it dry, and then repeat coat upon coat, until the color is sufficiently strong to show even and bright outside. Jars and vases may be decorated in endless variety by this method. Some use cuttings from prints, silks, &c.

New Method of Embalming.—Mix together five pounds dry sulphate of alumine, one quart of warm water, and one hundred grains of arsenious acid. Inject three or four quarts of this mixture into all the vessels of the human body. This applies as well to all animals, birds, fishes, &c. This process supersedes the old and revolting mode, and has been introduced into the great anatomical schools of Paris.

To Make Wax Flowers.—The following articles will be required to commence wax work: 2 pounds white wax, ¼ pound hair wire, 1 bottle carmine, 1 ultramarine blue, 1 bottle chrome yellow, 2 bottles chrome green, No. 1, 2 bottles chrome green, No. 2, 1 bottle rose pink, 1 bottle royal purple, 1 bottle scarlet powder, 1 bottle balsam fir, 2 dozen sheets white wax. This will do to begin with. Now have a clean tin dish and pour therein a quart or two of water; then put in about 1 pound of the white wax and let it boil; when cool enough, so the bubbles will not form on top, it is ready to sheet, which is done as follows:—Take half of a window pane, 7x9, and, after having washed it clean, dip into a dish containing weak soap-suds; then dip into the wax and draw out steadily and plunge it into the suds, when the sheet will readily come off. Lay it on a cloth or clean paper to dry. Proceed in like manner until you have enough of the white; then add enough of the green powder to make a bright color, and heat and stir thoroughly until the color is evenly distributed; then proceed as for sheeting white wax. The other colors are rubbed into the leaves after they are cut out, rubbing light or heavy according to shade.

For patterns you can use any natural leaf, forming the creases in wax with the thumb nail or a needle; to put the flowers together or the leaves onto the stem, hold in the hand until warm enough to stick. If the sheeted wax is to be used in summer, put in a little balsam of fir to make it hard. If for winter, none will be required.

You can make many flowers without a teacher; but one to assist in the commencement, would be a great help; though the most particular thing about it is to get the wax sheeted. The materials I have suggested can be procured at any drug store, and will cost from $3 to $4.50.

FARMERS' DEPARTMENT.

How to get New Varities of Potatoes.—When the vines are done growing and are turned brown; the seed is ripe; then take the balls and string with a large needle and strong thread; hang them in a dry place, where they will gradually dry and mature, without danger or injury from frost. In the month of April, soak the ball for several hours from the pulp, when washed and dried, they are fit for sowing in rows, in a bed well prepared in the garden; they will sprout in a fortnight; they must be attended to like other vegetables. When about two inches high, they may be thinned and transplanted into rows. As they increase in size, they should be hilled. In the autumn many of them will be the size of a walnut, and from that to a pea. In the following spring they should be planted in hills, placing the large ones together,—they will in the second season attain their full size, and will exhibit several varieties of form, and may then be selected to suit the judgment of the cultivater. I would prefer gathering the balls from potatoes of a good kind. The first crop from seeds thus obtained, will be productive, and will continue so for many years, gradually deteriorating, until they will need a renewal by the process.

To Destroy Rats.—Fill any deep smooth vessel of considerable capacity to within six inches of the top with water, cover the surface with bran, and set the vessel in a place most frequented by these pests. In attempting to get at the bran they will fall in and be drowned. Several dozen have been taken by this simple method at a time.

To Kill Rats in Barn and Rick.—Melt hogs lard in a bottle plunged in water of temperature of 150° Fahrenheit; introduced into it half an ounce of phosphorus for every pound of lard; then add a pint of proof spirits or whiskey; cork the bottle firmly after its contents have been to 150°, taking it out of the water and agitating till the phosphorus becomes uniformly diffused, making a milky looking fluid. The spirit may be poured off on the liquor cooling; and you then have a fatty compound, which after being warmed gently, may be incorporated with a mixture of wheat flower, or sugar, flavored with oil of rhodium, or oil of aniseseed, etc., and the dough, on being made into pellets, should be laid at the rat holes; being luminous in the dark and, agreeable both to the palates and noses, it is readily eaten, and proves certainly fatal. The rats issue from their holes and seek for water to quench their burning thirst, and they commonly die near the water.

Rat Poison.—Flour, six pounds; sugar, one pound; sulphur, four pounds; phosphorus, four pounds.

RECIPES FOR HORSES.

Blistering Liniment.—Powdered Spanish flies, one ounce; spirits turpentine, six ounces. Rub on the belly for pain in the bowels, or on the surface for internal inflammation.

Cathartic Powder.—To cleanse out horses in the spring, making them sleek and healthy; black sulphuret of antimony, nitre, and sulphur, each equal parts. Mix well together and give a tablespoonful every morning.

Cough Ball for Horses.—Pulverized ipecac, three quarters of an ounce; camphor, two ounces; squills, half an ounce. Mix with honey to form into a mass, and divide into eight balls. Give one every morning.

Diuretic Balls.—Castile soap scraped fine, powdered resin, each three teaspoonfuls; powdered nitre, four teaspoonfuls; oil of juniper, one small teaspoonful; honey, a sufficient quantity to make into a ball.

To Prevent Horses from Being Teased by Flies.—Boil three handfuls of walnut leaves in three quarts of water; sponge the horse (before going out of the stable) between and upon the ears, neck and flank.

To Prevent Botts.—Mix a little wood-ashes with their drink daily. This effectually preserves horses against the botts.

Liniment for Galled Backs of Horses.—White lead moistened with milk. When milk cannot be procured, oil may be substituted. One or two ounces will last two months or more.

Remedy for Strains in Horses.—Take whiskey, one half pint; camphor, one ounce; sharp vinegar, one pint. Mix. Bathe the parts affected.

Another.—Take opodeldoc, warm it, and rub the strained part two or three times a day.

Lotion for Blows, Bruises, Sprains, &c.—One part laudanum, two parts oil origanum, four parts water ammonia, four parts oil of turpentine, four parts camphor, thirty-two parts spirits of wine. Put them into a bottle, and shake them until mixed.

Fever Ball.—Emetic tartar and camphor, each half an ounce; nitre, two ounces. Mix with linseed meal and molasses to make eight balls. Give one twice a day.

Liniment for Sprains, Swellings, &c.—Aqua ammonia, spirits camphor, each two ounces; oil origanum, and laudanum, each half an ounce. Mix.

Lotion for Mange.—Boil two ounces tobacco in one quart water; strain; add sulphur and soft soap, each, two ounces.

Purgative Ball.—Aloes, one ounce; cream tartar and castile soap, one quarter of an ounce. Mix with molasses to make a ball.

CONFECTIONERS' DEPARTMENT.

Ginger Candy.—Boil a pound of clarified sugar until, upon taking out a drop of it on a piece of stick, it will become brittle when cold. Mix and stir up with it, for a common article, about a teaspoonful of ground ginger; if for a superior article, instead of the ground ginger add half the white of an egg, beaten up previously with fine sifted loaf sugar, and twenty drops of strong essence of ginger.

Another.—Take coarsely powdered ginger, two ounces; boiling water one and a quarter pints; macerate in a warm place for two hours, strain, and add seven pounds each of loaf and brown sugar.

Ginger Drops.—Are the same, except that they are made with all loaf sugar.

Ginger Lozenges.—Dissolve in one quarter of a pint of hot water half an ounce of gum arabic; when cold, stir it up with one and a half pounds of loaf sugar, and a spoonful of powdered ginger, or twelve drops of essence of ginger. Roll and beat the whole up into a paste; make it into a flat cake, and punch out the lozenges with a round stamp; dry them near the fire or in an oven.

Peppermint Lozenges.—Best powdered white sugar, seven lbs.; pure starch, one lb.; oil of peppermint to flavor. Mix with mucilage.

Peppermint, Rose or Hoarhound Candy.—They may be made as lemon candy. Flavor with essence of rose, or peppermint or finely powdered hoarhound. Pour it out in a buttered paper, placed in a square tin pan.

To Clarify Sugar for Candies.—To every pound of sugar, put a large cup of water, and put it in a brass or copper kettle, over a slow fire, for half an hour; pour into it a small quantity of isinglass and gum arabic, dissolved together. This will cause all impurities to rise to the surface; skim it as it rises. Flavor according to taste.

All kinds of sugar for candy, are boiled as above directed. When boiling loaf sugar, add a tablespoonful of rum or vinegar, to prevent its becoming too brittle whilst making.

Loaf sugar when boiled, by pulling and making into small rolls, and twisting a little, will make what is called little rock, or snow. By pulling loaf sugar after it is boiled, you can make it as white as snow.

Common Twist Candy,—Boil three pounds of common sugar and one pint of water over a slow fire for half an hour, without skimming. When boiled enough take it off; rub the hands over with butter, take that which is a little cooled, and pull it as you would molasses candy, until it is white; then twist or braid it, and cut it up in strips.

Fine Peppermint Lozenges.—Best powdered white sugar, seven pounds; pure starch, one pound; oil of peppermint to flavor. Mix with mucilage.

Everton Taffee.—To make this favorite and wholesome candy, take 1½ pounds of moist sugar, 3 ounces of butter, a teacup and a half of water and one lemon. Boil the sugar, butter, water, and half the rind of the lemon together, and when done—which will be known by dropping into cold water, when it should be quite crisp—let it stand aside till the boiling has ceased, and then stir in the juice of the lemon. Butter a dish, and pour it in about a quarter of an inch in thickness. The fire must be quick, and the taffee stirred all the time.

Candy Fruit.—Take 1 pound of the best loaf sugar; dip each lump into a bowl of water, and put the sugar into your preserving kettle. Boil it down and skim it until perfectly clear, and in a candying state. When sufficiently boiled, have ready the fruits you wish to preserve. Large white grapes, oranges separated into small pieces, or preserved fruits, taken out of their syrup and dried, are very nice. Dip the fruits into the prepared sugar while it is hot; put them in a cold place; they will soon become hard.

Popped Corn.—Dipped in boiling molasses and stuck together forms an excellent candy.

Liquorice Lozenges.—Extract of liquorice, 1 pound, powdered white sugar, 2 pounds. Mix with mucilage made with rosewater.

Fig Candy.—Take 1 pound of sugar and 1 pint of water, set over a slow fire. When done, add a few drops of vinegar and a lump of butter, and pour into pans in which split figs are laid.

Raisin Candy.—Can be made in the same manner, substituting stoned raisins for the figs. Common molasses candy is very nice with all kinds of nuts added.

Scotch Butter Candy.—Take 1 pound of sugar, 1 pint of water; dissolve and boil. When done add 1 tablespoonful of butter, and enough lemon juice and oil of lemon to flavor.

Icing for Cakes.—Beat the whites of two small eggs to a high froth; then add to them a quarter of a pound of white, ground or powdered sugar; beat it well until it will lie in a heap; flavor with lemon or rose. This will frost the top of a common-sized cake. Heap what you suppose to be sufficient in the centre of of the cake, then dip a broad-bladed knife in cold water, and spread the ice evenly over the whole surface.

Saffron Lozenges.—Finely powdered hay-saffron, one ounce; finely powdered sugar, one pound; finely powdered starch, eight ounces. Mucilage to mix.

Chocolate Cream.—Chocolate, scraped fine, $\frac{1}{2}$ ounce, thick cream, 1 pint; sugar, (best,) 3 ounces; heat it nearly to boiling, then remove it from the fire, and mill it well. When cold add the whites of four or five eggs; whisk rapidly and take up the froth on a sieve; serve the cream in glasses, and pile up the froth on the top of them.

Candied Lemon or Peppermint for Colds.—Boil 1½ pounds sugar in a half pint of water, till it begins to candy round the sides; put in eight drops of essence; pour it upon buttered paper, and cut it with a knife.

FOR THE HOUSEHOLD AND EVERY DAY REQUIREMENTS.

Alum in Starch.—For starching muslins, ginghams, and calicoes, dissolve a piece of alum the size of a shellbark, for every pint of starch, and add to it. By so doing the colors will keep bright for a long time, which is very desirable when dresses must be often washed, and the cost is but a trifle.

Cider Yeast.—Take cider from sour apples, before it ferments, scald, skim thoroughly, and pour, while hot, upon flour enough to make a stiff batter. When cool, add yeast of any kind, and let it rise, stirring it down as often as it tries to run over for several days, then put it in a cool place (where it will not freeze), and you will have something equal to the best hop yeast. It will keep until May without any further labor.

To Destroy Cockroaches.—The following is said to be effectual. These vermin are easily destroyed, simply by cutting up green cucumbers at night, and placing them about where roaches commit depredations. What is cut from the cucumbers in preparing them for the table answers the purpose as well, and three applications will destroy all the roaches in the house. Remove the peelings in the morning, and renew them at night.

Fire Kindlers.—Take a quart of tar and three pounds of resin, melt them, bring to a cooling temperature, mix with as much sawdust, with a little charcoal added, as can be worked in; spread out while hot upon a board, when cold break up into lumps of the size of a large hickory nut, and you have, at a small expense, kindling material enough for a household for one year. They will easily ignite from a match and burn with a strong blaze, long enough to start any wood that is fit to burn.

Remedy against Moths.—An ounce of gum camphor and one of the powdered shell of red pepper are macerated in eight ounces of strong alcohol for several days, then strained. With this tincture the furs or cloth are sprinkled over, and rolled up in sheets. Instead of the pepper, bitter apple may be used. This remedy is used in Russia under the name of the Chinese tincture of moths,

Substitute for Yeast.—Boil one pound of flour, one quarter pound of brown sugar and a little salt in two gallons of water for one hour. When milk-warm, bottle and cork close, and it will be ready for use in twenty-four hours.

To Make Lye.—Have a large tub or cask and bore a hole on one side for a tap, near the bottom; place several bricks near the hole and cover them with straw. Fill the barrel with strong wood ashes. Oak ashes are strongest, and those of apple tree wood make the whitest soap. Pour on boiling water until it begins to run, then put in the tap and let it soak. If the ashes settle down as they are wet, fill it until full.

Tomato Wine.—Take ripe fresh tomatoes, mash very fine, strain through a fine sieve, sweeten with good sugar, to suit the taste, set it away in an earthen or glass vessel, nearly full, cover tight, with exception of a small hole for the refuse to work off through during its fermentation. When it is done fermenting it will become pure and clear. Then bottle, and cork tight. A little salt improves its flavor; age improves it.

To Color Brown on Cotton or Woolen.—For ten pounds of cloth boil three pounds of catechu in as much water as needed to cover the goods. When dissolved, add four ounces of blue vitriol; stir it well; put in the cloth and let it remain all night; in the morning drain it thoroughly; put four ounces of bi-chromate of potash in boiling water sufficient to cover your goods; let it remain fifteen minutes; wash in cold water; color in iron.

To Cleanse and Brighten Faded Brussels Carpet.—Boil some bran in water and with this wash the carpet with a flannel and brush, using Fuller's earth for the worst parts. When dry the carpet must be well beaten to get out the fuller's earth, then washed over with a weak solution of alum to brighten the colors. Some housekeepers cleanse and brighten carpets by sprinkling them first with fine salt and then sweeping them thoroughly.

To give Stoves a fine Brilliant Appearance.—A teaspoonful of pulverized alum mixed with stove polish will give the stove a fine lustre, which will be quite permanent.

Method of Keeping Hams in Summer.—Make bags of unbleached muslin; place in the bottom a little good sweet hay; put in the ham, and then press around and over it firmly more hay; tie the bag and hang up in a dry place. Ham secured in this way will keep for years.

How to Cause Vegetables and Fruits to Grow to an Enormous Size and also to Increase the Brilliancy and Fragrancy of Flowers.—A curious discovery has recently been made public in France, in regard to the culture of vegetable and fruit trees. By watering with a solution of sulphate of iron, the most wonderful fecundity has been attained. Pear-trees and beans, which have been submitted to this treatment, have nearly doubled in the size of their productions, and a noticeable improvement has been remarked in their flavor. Dr. Becourt reports that while at the head of an establishment at Enghien, or the sulphurous springs, he had the gardens and plantations connected with it watered, during several weeks of the early spring, with sulphurous water, and not only the plantations prospered to a remarkable extent, but flowers acquired a peculiar brilliancy of coloring and healthy aspect which attracted universal attention.

Drying Corn.—With a sharp knife shave the corn from the ear, then scrape the cob, leaving one-half the hull clinging to the cob. Place a tin or earthen vessel two-thirds full of this "milk of corn" over a kettle of boiling water, stir frequently until dry enough to spread upon a firm cloth without sticking, when the wind and sun (away from dust and flies) will soon complete the process. To prepare for the table, put in cold water, set it where it will become hot, but not boil, for two hours; then season with salt and pepper, boil for ten minutes; add of butter and white sugar a tablespoonful of each just before ready to serve.

To Destroy Lice on Chickens.—The following will kill lice on the first application: Put six cents worth of cracked *Coculus Indicus* berries into a bottle that will hold a half pint of alcohol; fill the bottle with alcohol, and let it stand twenty-four hours. When the hen comes off with the young chickens, take the mixture, and with a small cotton rag, wet the head of each chicken enough to have it reach through the little feathers to the skin; also with the same rag, wet the hen under her wings. Be careful that no child, nor any one else, uses it, because it is a *deadly poison.*

Cracked Wheat.—For a pint of the cracked grain, have two quarts of water boiling in a smooth iron pot over a quick fire; stir in the wheat slowly; boil fast and stir constantly for the first half hour cooking, or until it begins to thicken and "pop up;" then lift from the quick fire, and place the pot where the wheat will cook slowly for an hour longer. Keep it covered closely, stir now and then, and be careful not to let it burn at the bottom. Wheat cooked thus is much sweeter and richer than when left to soak and simmer for hours, as many think necessary. White wheat cooks the easiest. When ready to dish out, have your moulds moistered with cold water, cover lightly, and set in a cool place. Eat warm or cold with milk and sugar.

How to have Green Pea Soup in Winter.—Sow peas thickly in pots and boxes, say six weeks before the soup is wanted. Place them in a temperature of 60° or so, close to the glass in a house or pit. Cut the plants as soon as they attain a height of from three to six inches, and rub them through a sieve. The shoots alone will make a fair soup. Mixed with dry peas, also passed through a sieve, no one could scarcely distinguish color or flavor from that of real green pea soup. There is, however, considerable difference in the flavor of pea leaves, as well as of the peas themselves. The best marrows, such as Ne Plus Ultra and Veitche's Perfection, yield the most piquant cuttings. Also the more light the plants receive the higher the flavor, plants drawn up or at all blanched, being by no means comparable with those well and strongly grown.

In the spring, a few patches or rows may be sown in open quarters expressly for green cuttings. These are most perfect and full flavored when four inches high. When too long the flavor seems to have run to wood, and the peculiar aroma of green peas is weaker.

There is yet another mode of making green pea soup at any season at very short notice. Chip the peas by steeping them in water and leaving them in a warm place for a few days. Then slightly boil or stew, chips and all, and pass them through a sieve. The flavor is full and good, though such pea soup lacks color. It is astonishing how much the mere vegetation of seeds develops their more active and predominant flavor or qualities;

a fact that might often be turned to useful account in the kitchen in flavoring of soups or dishes, with turnips, celery, parsley, &c.

Composition for Restoring Scorched Linen.—Boil, to a good consistency, in half a pint of vinegar, two ounces of Fuller's earth, an ounce of hen's dung, half an ounce of cake soap, and the juice of two onions. Spread this composition over the whole of the damaged part; and if the scorching is not quite through, and the threads actually consumed, after suffering it to dry on, and letting it receive a subsequent good washing or two, the place will appear full as white and perfect as any other part of the linen.

To Remove Indelible Ink Stains.—Soak the stained spot in strong salt water, then wash it with ammonia. Salt changes the nitrate of silver into chloride of silver, and ammonia dissolves the chloride.

To Cook Cauliflower.—Choose those that are close and white and of middle size, trim off the outside leaves, cut the stalk off flat at the bottom, let them lie in salt and water an hour before you boil them. Put them into boiling water with a handful of salt in it, skim it well and let it boil slowly till done. Fifteen minutes will suffice for a small one, and twenty will be long enough for a large one. If it is boiled a minute or two after it is done the flavor will be impaired.

To Pickle String Beans.—Place them in a pan with alternate layers of salt and leave them thus for twenty-four hours. Drain them and place them in a jar with allspice, cloves, pepper, and a little salt. Boil enough vinegar to cover them, pour over them and let them stand till the next day, boil the vinegar the second time, and pour it on again. The next day boil the vinegar for the last time, pour it over the beans, and when quite cold, cover the jar tightly and set in a cool closet.

Chili Sauce.—Twelve ripe tomatoes, four ripe peppers, two onions, two tablespoofuls of salt, two tablespoonfuls of sugar, three tea-cups of vinegar, a little cinnamon; peel the tomatoes and chop them fine, also the peppers and onions, and boil all together one hour.

How to Cause a Baby to Thrive and Grow.—Try the milk first drawn from a cow that is fresh, add one-quarter water, and a little sugar. If the milk constipates, sweeten it with molasses, or mix with it a small quantity of magnesia. Abjure soothing syrups, and for colic give catnip or smellage tea. Give the baby a tepid bath at night as well as in the morning, rubbing him well with the hand. After the bath, let him feed and then sleep, We find open air the best tonics for babies. Ours takes his naps out of doors in the shade during the warm weather, and his cheeks are two roses.

To Can Gooseberries without Breaking them.—Fill the cans with berries, and partly cover with water, set the jars into a vessel of water, and raise the temperature to the boiling point. Boil eight minutes, remove from the kettle, cover with boiling water, and seal immediately. If sugar is used, let it be pure white, and allow eight ounces to a quart of berries. Make into a syrup, and use in the cans instead of water. The glass cans with glass tops, a rubber and a screw ring, we have found the simplest and most perfect of the many kinds offered for sale in the market.

Ready Mode of Mending Cracks in Stoves, Pipes, and Iron Ovens. —When a crack is discovered in a stove, through which the fire or smoke penetrates, the aperture may be completely closed in a moment with a composition consisting of wood ashes and common salt, made up into paste with a little water, and plastered over the crack. The good effect is equally certain, whether the stove, etc., be cold or hot.

Preservation of Milk and Cream.—Put the milk into bottles, then place them in a saucepan with cold water, and gradually raise it to the boiling point; take it from the fire, [and instantly cork the bottles, then raise the milk once more to the boiling point for half a minute. Finally let the bottles cool in the water in which they were boiled. Milk thus treated will remain perfectly good for six months. Emigrants, especially those having children will find the above hint add much to their comfort while on their voyage.

To Keep Milk from Turning Sour.—Add a little sub-carbonate of soda, or of potash. This by combining with, and neutralizing the acetic acid formed, has the desired effect, and keeps the milk from turning sooner than it otherwise would. The addition is perfectly harmless, and does not injure the taste.

Strawberry Vinegar.—Put four pounds of very ripe strawberries, nicely dressed, into three quarts of the best vinegar, and let them stand three or four days; then drain the vinegar through a jelly-bag, and pour it on the same quantity of fruit. Repeat the process in the days for a third time. Finally, to each pound of the liquor thus obtained, add one pound of fine sugar. Bottle, and let it stand covered, but not tightly corked, one week; then cork it tight, and set it in a cool, *dry* place, where it will not freeze. Raspberry vinegar is made the same way.

Cider Vinegar.—After cider has become too sour for use, set it in a warm place, put to it occasionally the rinsings of the sugar basin or molasses jug, and any remains of ale or cold tea; let it remain with the bung open, and you will soon have the best of vinegar.

To give Lustre to Silver.—Dissolve a quantity of alum in water, so as to make a pretty strong brine, and skim it carefully; then add some soap to it, and dip a linen rag in it, and rub over the silver.

To make Water-Proof Porous Cloth.—Close water-proof cloth fabrics, such as glazed oil-cloth, Indian-rubber, and guttapercha cloth are completely water-proof, put do not permit perspiration and the exhalted gases from the skin to pass through them, because they are air-tight as well as water-tight. Persons who wear air-tight garments soon become faint, if they are undergoing severe exercise, such as that to which soldiers are exposed when on march. A porous, water-proof cloth, therefore, is the best for outer garments during wet weather, for those whose duties or labor causes them to prespire freely. The best way for preparing such cloth is by the following process: Take 2¼ lbs. of alum and dissolve this in 10 gallons of boiling water; then in a separate vessel dissolve the same quantity of sugar of lead in 10 gallons of water, and mix the two solutions. The cloth is now well handled in this liquid, until every part of it is penetrated; then it is squeezed and dried in the air, or in a warm apartment, then washed in cold water and dried again, when it is fit for use. If necessary, the cloth may be dipped in the liquid and dried twice before being washed. The liquor appears curdled, when the alum and lead solutions are mixed together. This is the result of double decomposition, the sulphate of lead, which is an insoluble salt, being formed. The sulphate of lead is **taken up in the pores of the cloth, and it is unaffected by rains** or moisture, and yet it does not render the cloth air-tight. Such cloth is also partially non-inflammable. A solution of alum itself will render cloth, prepared as described, partially waterproof, but it is not so good as the sulphate of lead. Such cloth —cotton or woolen—sheds rain like the feathers on the back of a duck.

To Cleanse Carpet.—1 teaspoonful liquid ammonia in 1 gallon warm water, will often restore the color of carpets, even if produced by acid or alkali. If a ceiling has been whitewashed with carpet down, and a few drops are visible, this will remove it. Or, after the carpet is well beaten and brushed, scour it with oxgall, which will not only extract grease but freshen the colors— 1 pint of gall in three gallons of warm water, will do a large carpet. Table floor-cloths may be thus washed. The suds left from a wash where ammonia is used, even if almost cold, cleanses these floor-cloths well.

To Keep Hams.—After the meat has been well cured by pickle and smoke, take some clean ashes from bits of coal; moisten them with a little water so that they will form a paste, or else just wet the hams a little, and rub on the dry ashes. Rubbed in thoroughly they serve as a capital insect protector, and the hams can be hung up in the smoke-house or wood-chamber without any danger of molestation.

A Cold Cement for Mending Earthenware, says a recent English work, reckoned a great secret among workmen, is made by grating a pound of old cheese, with a bread grater, into a quart of milk, in which it must be left for a period of fourteen hours. It should be stirred quite often. A pound of unslaked lime, finely pulverized in a mortar, is then added, and the whole is thoroughly mixed by beating. This done, the whites of twenty-five eggs are incorporated with the rest, and the whole is ready for use. There is another cement for the same purpose which is used hot. It is made of resin, beeswax, brick dust, and chalk boiled together. The substances to be cemented must be heated, and when the surfaces are coated with cement, they must be rubbed hard upon each other, as in making a glue joint with wood.

How to Make Cucumber Vines Bear Five Crops.—When a cucumber is taken from the vine let it be cut with a knife leaving about the eight of an inch of the cucumber on the stem, then slit the stem with a knife from the end to the vine, leaving a small portion of the cucumber on each division, and on each separate slit there will be a new cucumber as large as the first·

White Cement.—Take white (fish) glue, 1 lb. 10 oz., dry white lead 6 oz.; soft water 3 pints; alcohol 1 pint.

Dissolve the glue by putting it in a tin kettle or dish, containing the water, and set this dish in a kettle of water, to prevent the glue from being burned; when the glue is all dissolved, put in the lead and stir and boil until it is thoroughly mixed; remove from the fire, and when cool enough to bottle, add the alcohol, and bottle while it is yet warm, keeping it corked. This last recipe has been sold about the country for from twenty-five cents to five dollars, and one man gave a horse for it.

To Clean Furniture.—An old cabinet maker says the best preparation for cleaning picture frames and restoring furniture, especially that somewhat marred or scratched, is a mixture of three parts linseed oil and one part spirits ot turpentine. It not only covers the disfigured surface, but restores wood to its natural color, and leaves a lustre upon its surface. Put on with a woolen cloth, and when dry, rub with woolen.

Bruises on Furniture.—Wet the part in warm water; double a piece of brown paper five or six times, soak in the warm water, and lay it on the place, apply on that a warm, but not hot, flat-iron till the moisture is evaporated. If the bruise be not gone repeat the process. After two or three applications the dent will be raised to the surface. If the bruise be small, merely soak it with warm water, and hold a red-hot iron near the surface keeping the surface continually wet—the bruise will soon disappear.

To Prevent Iron Rust.—Kerosene applied to stoves or farming implements, during summer, will prevent their rusting.

To Color Sheep Skins.—Unslaked lime and litharge equal parts, mixed to a thin paste with water, will color buff—several coats will make it a dark brown; by adding a little ammonia and nitrate of silver a fine black is produced. Terra japonica will impart a "tan color" to wool, and the red shade is deepened by sponging with a solution of lime and water, using a strong solution of alum water to "set" the colors; 1 part crystalized nitrate silver, 8 parts carbonate ammonia, and 1½ parts of soft water dyes brown; every additional coat darkens the color until a black is obtained.

Remedy for Burns.—Take one teacup of lard and the whites of two eggs; work together as much as it can be, then spread on cloths and apply. Change as often as necessary.

How Summer Suits should be Washed.—Summer suits are nearly all made of white or buff linen, pique, cambric, or muslin, and the art of preserving the new appearance after washing is a matter of the greatest importance. Common washwomen spoil everything with soda, and nothing is more frequent than to see the delicate tints of lawns and percales turned into dark blotches and muddy streaks by the ignorance and vandalism of a laundress. It is worth while for ladies to pay attention to this, and insist upon having their summer dresses washed according to the directions which they should be prepared to give their laundresses themselves. In the first place, the water should be tepid, the soap should not be allowed to touch the fabric; it should be washed and rinsed quick, turned upon the wrong side, and hung in the shade to dry, and when starched (in thin boiled but not boiling starch) should be folded in sheets or towels, and ironed upon the wrong side as soon as possible. But linen should be washed in water in which hay or a quart bag of bran has been boiled. This last will be found to answer for starch as well, and is excellent for pink dresses of all kinds, but a handful of salt is very useful also to set the colors of light cambrics and dotted lawns; and a little ox gall will not only set but brighten yellow and purple tints, and has a good affect upon green.

How to Fasten Rubber to Wood and Metal.—As rubber plates and rings are now-a-days used almost exclusively for making connections between steam and other pipes and apparatus, much annoyance is often experienced by the impossibility or imperfection of an air-tight connection. This is obviated entirely by employing a cement which fastens alike well to the rubber and to the metal or wood. Such cement is prepared by a solution of shellac in ammonia. This is best made by soaking pulverized gum shellac in ten times its weight of strong ammonia, when a slimy mass is obtained, which in three or four weeks will become liquid without the use of hot water. This softens the rubber, and becomes, after volatilization of the ammonia, hard and impermeable to gases and fluids.

Renewing Maroon Colors on Wool.—Wash the goods in very weak lye; then rinse thoroughly in clear water; thus you have a beautiful, *even* color, although your goods have been much faded and stained. Though the color thus obtained may not be the exact shade as when new, it is, however, a very pretty one. The above will not answer for other than all woolen goods of a maroon color.

To make Water-Proof Cloth out of thick Ducking.—The following French recipe is given: Take two pounds four ounces of alum, and dissolve it in ten gallons of water. In like manner dissolve the same quantity of sugar of lead in a similar quantity of water, and mix the two together. They form a precipitate of the sulphate of lead. The clear liquor is now withdrawn, and the cloth immersed one hour in the solution, when it is taken out and dried in the shade, washed in clean water and dried again.

Cochineal Coloring.—The following is a good recipe:—Cochineal, alum, cream tartar carb. potassa, each three drachms; water, eight ounces; sugar six ounces. Rub the cochineal, alum and cream tartar, with eight ounces boiling water, and, when cold, gradually add carb. potassa, and strain; pour water on the strainer sufficient to measure eight fluid ounces, then add the sugar.

How to Stop a Pinhole in Lead Pipe.—Take a ten-penny nail, place the square end upon the hole, and hit it two or three slight blows with s hammer, and the orifice is closed as tight as though you had employed a plumber to do it at a cost of a dollar or more.

To Build a Chimney that Will Not Smoke.—The *Scientific American* gives the following hints to those who would "build a chimney that would not smoke:"—The chief point is to make the throat not less than four inches broad and 12 long; then the chimney should be abruptly enlarged to double the size, and so continue for one foot or more; then it may be gradually tapered off as desired. But the inside of the chimney throughout its whole length to the top, should be plastered very smooth with good mortar, which will harden with age. The area of a chimney should be at least half a square foot, and no flues less than sixty square inches. The best shape for a chimney is circular, or many-sided, as giving less friction, (brick is the best material as it is a non-conductor,) and the higher above the roof the better.

To Prevent Turners' Wood Splitting.—Small pieces of valuable wood, such kinds as are used for turning, etc., are very liable to split readily—that is, outward from the centre. To prevent this, soak the pieces, when first cut, in *cold* water for twenty-four hours, then boil in hot water for two or three hours, and afterward dry slowly, and under cover. This will be found useful in making handsome mantle, toilet, and other articles from sumac, cherry, and other woods that never grow very large.

To remove Dry Paint on Windows.—The most economical way to remove dry paint from the panes is to make a small swab having a handle some eight inches long, dip it in a little diluted oxalic acid, and rub off the paint with a swab.

Everlasting Fence Posts.—I discovered many years ago that wood could be made to last longer than iron in the ground but thought the process so simple and inexpensive that it was not worth while making any stir about it. I would as soon have poplar, basswood, or quaking ash as any other kind of timber for fence posts. I have taken out basswood posts after having been set seven years, which were as sound when taken out as when they were first put in the ground. Time and weather seemed to have no effect on them. The posts can be prepared for less than two cents a piece. This is the recipe: Take boiled linseed oil and stir it in pulverized charcoal to the consistency of paint. Put a coat of this over the timber, and there is not a man who will live to see it rotten.

How to Test the Richness of Milk.—Procure any long glass vessel—a cologne bottle or long phial. Take a narrow strip of paper, just the length from the neck to the bottom of the phial, and mark it off with one hundred lines at equal distances; or fifty lines, and count each as two, and paste it upon the phial, so as to divide its length into a hundred equal parts. Fill it to the highest mark with milk fresh from the cow, and allow it to stand in a perpendicular position twenty-four hours. The number of spaces occupied by the cream will give you its exact precentage in the milk without any guess work.

To Mend Tinware by the heat of a Candle.—Take a vial about two-thirds full of muriatic acid, and put into it little bits of sheet zinc as long as it dissolves them; then put in a crump of sal-ammoniac, and fill it up with water, and it is ready for use.

Then, with the cork of the vial, wet the place to be mended with the preparation; then put a piece of sheet zinc over the hole, and hold a lighted candle or spirit-lamp under the place, which melts the solder on the tin, and causes the zinc to adhere without further trouble. Wet the zinc also with the solution; or a little solder may be put on instead of the zinc, or with the zinc.

To Remove Stains.—The stains of ink on cloth, paper, or wood may be removed by almost all acids; but those acids are to be preferred which are least likely to injure the texture of the stained substance. The muriatic acid, diluted with five or six times its weight of water, may be applied to the spot, and after a minute or two may be washed off, repeating the application as often as may be necessary. But the vegetable acids are attended with less risk, and are equally effected. A solution of the oxalic, citric (acid of lemons), or tartareous acids in water may be applied to the most delicate fabrics, without any danger of injuring them; and the same solutions will discharge writing but not printing ink. Hence they may be applied in cleaning books which have been defaced by writing on the margin, without imparing the text. Lemon-juice and the juice of sorrels will also remove ink-stains, but not so easily as the concrete acid of lemons or citric acid.

To Prevent Snow-water or Rain from Penetrating the Soles of Shoes or Boots in Winter.—This simple and effectual remedy is nothing more than a little beeswax and mutton suet, warmed in a pipkin until in a liquid state. Then rub some of it lightly over the edges of the sole where the stiches are, which will repel the wet, and not in the least prevent the blacking from having the usual effect.

An Easy Method of preventing Moths in Furs or Woolens.—Sprinkle the furs or woolen stuffs, as well as the drawers or boxes in which they are kept, with spirits of turpentine; the unpleasant scent of which will speedily evaporate on exposure of the stuffs to the air. Some people place sheets of paper, moistened with spirits of turpentine, over, under, or between pieces of cloth, etc., and find it a very effectual mode.

To keep Moths, Beetles, etc., from Clothes.—Put a piece of camphor in a linen-bag, or some aromatic herbs, in the drawers, among linen or woolen clothes, and neither moth nor worm will come near them.

To make Sea-water fit for Washing Linen at Sea.—Soda put into sea-water renders it turbid: the lime and magnesia fall to the bottom. To make sea-water fit for washing linen at sea, as much soda must be put in it, as not only to effect a complete precipitation on these earths, but to render the sea-water sufficiently laxivial or alkaline. Soda should always be taken to sea for this purpose.

To Destroy Insects.—When bugs have obtained a lodgment in walls or timber, the surest mode of overcoming the nuisance is to putty up every hole is moderately large, and oil-paint the whole wall or timber. In bed-furniture, a mixture of soft soap, with snuff or arsenic, is useful to fill up the holes where the bolts or fastenings are fixed, etc. French polish may be applied to smoother parts of the wood.

Poultice for Burns and Frozen Flesh.—Indian-meal poultices, covered with young hyson tea; moistened with hot water, and laid over burns or frozen parts, as hot as can be borne, will relieve the pain in five minutes, and blisters, if they have not, will not arise. One poultice is usually sufficient.

Cracked Nipples.—Glycerine and tannin, equal weights, rubbed together into an ointment, is highly recommended, as is also mutton tallow and glycerine.

To take the Impression of any Butterfly in all its Colors.—Having taken a butterfly, kill it without spoiling its wings, which contrive to spread out as regularly as possible in a flying position. Then, with a small brush or pencil, take a piece of white paper; wash part of it with gum-water, a little thicker than ordinary, so that it may easily dry. Afterwards, laying your butterfly on the paper, cut off the body close to the wings, and, throwing it away, lay the paper on a smooth board with the fly upwards; and, laying another paper over that, put the while preparation into a screw-press, and screw down very hard, letting it remain under that pressure for half an hour. Afterwards take off the wings of the butterfly and you will find a perfect impression of them, with all their various colors, marked distinctly, remaining on the paper. When this is done draw between the wings of your impression the body of the butterfly, and color it after the insect itself.

To take the Stains of Grease from Woolen or Silk.—Three ounces of spirits of wine, three ounces of French chalk powdered, and five ounces of pipe-clay. Mix the above ingredients, and make them up in rolls about the length of a finger, and you will find a never-failing remedy for removing grease from woollen or silken goods. N. B.—It is applied by rubbing on the spot either dry or wet, and afterwards brushing the place.

Easy and Safe Method of discharging Grease from Woollen Cloths. —Fuller's earth and tobacco pipe-clay, being put wet on an oil-spot, absorbs the oil as the water evaporates, and leaves the vegetable or animal fibres of the cloth clean on being beaten or brushed out. When the spot is occasioned by tallow or wax, it is necessary to heat the part cautiously by an iron or the fire while the cloth is drying. In some kind of goods, blotting-paper, bran, or raw starch, may be used with advantage.

To Take out Spots of Ink.—As soon as the accident happens, wet the place with juice of sorrel or lemen, or with vinegar, and the best hard white soap.

To take Iron-moulds out of Linen.—Hold the iron-mould on the cover of a tankard of boiling water, and rub on the spot a little juice of sorrel and a little salt; and when the cloth has thoroughly imbibed the juice, wash it in lye.

To take out Spots on Silk.—Rub the spots with spirits of turpentine, this spirit exhaling, carries off with it the oil that causes the spot.

To take Wax out of Velvet of all Colors except Crimson.—Take a crumby wheaten loaf, cut in two, toast it before the fire, and, while very hot, apply it to the part spotted with wax. Then apply another piece of toasted bread hot as before, and continue this application until the wax is entirely taken out.

To Bleach Straw.—Straw is bleached by the vapors of sulphur, or a solution of oxalic acid or chloride of lime. It may be dyed with any liquid color.

Windows, to Crystallize.—Dissolve epsom-salts in hot ale, or solution of gum arabic, wash it over the window, and let it dry. If you wish to remove any, to form a border or centre-piece, do it with a wet cloth.

Wax for Bottling.—Rosin, 13 parts; wax, 1 part, melt and add any color. Used to render corks and bungs air-tight by *melting the wax* over them.

Whitewash.—Slack half a bushel of lime with boiling water, and cover the vessel to retain the steam. Strain the liquor, and add one peck of salt previously dissolved in warm water, 3 lbs. of rice boiled and ground to a paste, Spanish whiting, 8 oz.; glue, 1 pound; mix and add hot water, 5 gallons; let it stand a few days, and apply hot. It makes a brilliant wash for inside or outside works.

To Purify Water for Drinking.—Filter river-water through a sponge, more or less compressed, instead of stone or sand, by which the water is not only rendered more clean, but wholesome; for sand is insensibly dissolved by the water, so that in four or five years it will have lost a fifth part of its weight. Powder of charcoal should be added to the sponge when the water is foul or fetid. Those who examine the large quantity of terrene matter on the inside of tea-kettles, will be convinced all water should be boiled before drinking, if they wish to avoid being affected with gravel or stone, etc.

To Purify the Muddy Waters of Rivers or Pits.—Make a number of holes in the bottom of a deep tub; lay some clean gravel thereon, and above this some clean sand; sink this tub in the river or pit, so that only a few inches of the tub will be above the surface of the water; the river or pit water will filter through the sand, and rise clear through it to the level of the water on the outside, and will be pure and limpid.

Method of Making Putrid Water Sweet in a Night's Time.—Four large spoonfuls of unslacked lime, put into a puncheon of ninety gallons of putrid water at sea, will, in one night, make it as clear and sweet as the best spring-water just drawn; but unless the water is afterwards ventilated sufficiently to carbonize the lime, it will be lime-water. Three ounces of pure unslacked lime should saturate 90 gallons of water.

Tree of Lead.—Dissolve an ounce of sugar of lead in a quart of clean water, and put it into a glass decanter or globe. Then suspend in the solution, near the top, a small piece of zinc of an irregular shape. Let it stand undisturbed for a day, and it will begin to shoot out into leaves, and apparently to vegetate. If left undisturbed for a few days, it will become extremely beautiful; but it must be moved with great caution. It may appear to those unacquainted with chemistry, that the piece of zinc actually puts out leaves; but this is a mistake, for, if the zinc be examined, it will be found nearly unaltered. This phenomenon is owing to the zinc having a greater attraction for oxygen than the lead has; consequently, it takes it from the oxide of lead, which re-appears in its metallic state.

Arbor Martis, or Tree of Mars.—Dissolve iron filings in acquafortis moderately concentrated, till the acid is saturated; then add to it gradually a solution of mixed alkali, commonly called oil of tartar per deliquium. A strong effervescence will ensue; and the iron, instead of falling to the bottom of the vessel, will afterwards rise so as to cover the sides, forming a multitude of ramifications heaped one upon the other, which will sometimes pass over the edge of the vessel, and extend themselves on the outside with all the appearance of a plant.

To keep Apples from Freezing.—Apples form an article of chief necessity in almost every family: therefore, great care is taken to keep them from frost; it being well known that they, if left unprotected, are destroyed by the first frost which occurs. They may be kept in the attic with impunity throughout the winter, by simply covering them over with a linen cloth: be sure to have *linen*, for woolen or other cloth is of *no avail*.

To Preserve Grapes.—Take a cask or barrel which will hold water, and put into it, first a layer of bran, dried in an oven or of ashes well dried and sifted, upon this place a layer of grapes well cleaned, and gathered in the afternoon of a dry day, before they are perfectly ripe; proceed thus with alternate layers of bran or ashes and grapes, till the barrel is full, taking care that the grapes do not touch each other, and to let the last layer be of bran or ashes, then close the barrel so that the air may not penetrate, which is an essential point. Grapes thus packed will keep for nine or even twelve months. To restore them to freshness, cut the end of the stalk of each bunch of grapes, and put it into red wine, as you would flowers into water. White grapes should be put into white wine.

To Increase the Laying of Eggs.—The best method is to mix with their food, every other day, about a teaspoon of ground cayenne pepper to each dozen fowl. Whilst upon this subject, it would be well to say, that if your hens lay soft eggs, or eggs without shells, you should put plenty of old plaster, egg-shells, or even oyster-shells broken up, where they can get at it.

To Preserve Meats.—Beef to pickle for long keeping. First, thoroughly rub salt into it, and let it remain in bulk for twenty-four hours to draw off the blood. Second, take it up, letting it drain, and pack as desired. Third, have ready a pickle prepared as follows: for every 100 pounds of beef use 7 pounds salt; saltpetre and cayenne pepper each, 1 ounce; molasses, 1 quart; and soft water, 8 gallons; boil and skim well, and when cold pour over the beef.

Another method is to use 5 pounds salt, 1 pound brown sugar, and $\frac{1}{4}$ ounce saltpetre, to each 100 pounds; dissolve the above in sufficient water to cover the meat, and in two weeks drain all off, and make more same as first. It will then keep through the season. To boil for eating, put into boiling water; for soups, into cold water.

Flies, to Destroy.—Boil some quassia-chips in a little water, sweeten with syrup or molasses, and place it in saucers. It is destructive to flies, but not to children.

Walnuts to Pickle.—Take 100 young walnuts, lay them in salt and water for two or three days, changing the water every day. (If required to be soon ready for use, pierce each walnut with a larding pin that the pickle may penetrate.) Wipe them with a soft cloth, and lay them on a folded cloth for some hours. Then put them in a jar, and pour on them sufficient of the above spiced vinegar, hot, to cover them. Or they may be allowed to simmer gently in strong vinegar, then put into a jar with a handful of mustard-seed, 1 ounce of ginger, $\frac{1}{4}$ ounce mace, 1 ounce allspice, 2 heads of garlic, and 2 split nutmegs; and pour on them sufficient boiling vinegar to cover them. Some prefer the walnuts to be gently simmered with the brine, then laid on a cloth for a day or two till they turn black, put into a jar, and hot spiced vinegar poured on them.

To Pickle Cucumbers and Gherkins.—Small cucumbers, but not too young, are wiped clean with a dry cloth, put into a jar, and boiling vinegar, with a handful of salt, poured on them. Boil up the vinegar every three days, and pour it on them until they become green; then add ginger and pepper, and tie them up close for use, or cover them with salt and water (as above) in a stone jar; cover them, and set them on the hearth before the fire for two or three days, till they turn yellow; then put away the water, and cover them with hot vinegar, set them near the fire, and keep them hot for eight or ten days, till they become green; then pour off the vinegar, cover them with hot spiced vinegar, and cover them close.

Mushroom Ketchup.—Pickled mushrooms, 4 pounds; salt, 2 pounds. Sprinkle it on the mushrooms; and, when they liquefy, remove the juice; add pimento, 6 ounces; cloves, 1 ounce; boil gently and strain; the remaining liquor, if any, may be treated with pepper, mace, and ginger for a second quality.

Tomato Ketchup.—Proceed as for mushroom ketchup, and add a little Chili pepper vinegar.

Court-plaster.—Court-plaster is made by repeatedly brushing over stretched sarcenet with a solution of 1 part of isinglass in 8 of water mixed with 8 parts of proof spirit, and finishing with a coat of tincture of benzoin, or of balsam of Peru.

Eye-water.—Extract of lead, 2 drachms; wine of digitalis 1 drachm tincture of opium, 2 drachms; water a pint.

Godfrey's Cordial.—The Philadelphia College of Pharmacy, to prevent the mischief arising from the different strengths of this compound, directs it to be prepared as follows:—Dissolve 2½ oz. of carbonate of potash in 26 pints of water, add 16 pints of treacle, heat together over a gentle fire till they simmer, remove the scum, and, when sufficiently cool, add ½ oz. of oil of sassafras dissolved in two pints of rectified spirit, and 24 fluid ounces of tincture of opium previously mixed. The old wine measure is here intended. It contains about 16 minims of laudanum, or rather more than 1 grain of opium in each fluid ounce.

Godfrey's Smelling-salts.—Dr. Paris says it is prepared by resubliming volatile salt swith sub-carbonate of potash and a little spirit of wine. It is usually scented with an alcoholic solution of essential oils.

Stoughton's Elixir.—Gentian, 36 oz.; serpentary, 16 oz., dried orange-peel, 24 oz.; calamus aromaticus, 4 oz.; rectified spirit and water, of each 6 galls., old measure.

Dr. Latham's Cough-linctus.—Dover's powder, ½ dr.; compound powder of tragacanth, 2 dr.; syrup of tolu, ½ ounce; confection of hips and simple oxymel, of each 1 ounce; a teaspoonful 3 or 4 times a day.

Morrison's Pills.—Consist of 2 parts of gamboge, 3 of aloes, 1 of colocynth, and 4 of cream of tartar; made into pills with syrup.

CALICO PRINTERS' FAST DYES.

Dye-stuffs used by calico-printers for producing fast colors.—The mordants are thickened with gum, or calcined starch, when applied with the block, rollers, plates, or pencil.

Black.—The cloth is impregnated with acetate of iron (iron liquor), and died in a bath of madder and logwood.

Purple.—The preceding mordant of iron, diluted; with the same dyeing bath.

Crimson.—The mordant for purple, united with a portion of acetate of alumina, or red mordant, and the above bath.

Red.—Acetate of alumina is the mordant, and madder is the dye-stuff.

Pale Red of different shades.—The preceding mordant, diluted with water, and a weak madder bath.

Brown, or Pompadour.—A mixed mordant, containing a somewhat larger proportion of the red than of the black, and the dye of madder.

Orange.—The red mordant; and a bath, first of madder, and then of quercitron.

Yellow.—A strong red mordant; and the quercitron bath, whose temperature should be considerably under the boiling point of water.

Blue.—Indigo, rendered soluble and greenish-yellow colored, by potash and orpiment. It recovers its blue color by exposure to air, and thereby also fixes firmly on the cloth. An indigo vat is also made, with that blue substance diffused in water with quicklime and copperas. These substances are supposed to deoxidize indigo, and at the same time to render it soluble.

Golden-dye.—The cloth is immersed alternately in a solution of copperas and lime-water. The protoxide of iron precipitated on the fiber, soon passes, by absorption of atmospherical oxygen, into the golden-colored deutoxide.

Buff.—The preceding substances iy a more diluted state.

Blue Vats.—In which white spots are left on a blue ground of cloth, is made by applying to those points a paste composed of a solution of sulphate of copper and pipe-clay, and after they are dried, immersing it, stretched on frames, for a definite number of minutes, in the yellowish green vat, of 1 part of indigo, 2 of copperas, and 2 of lime, with water.

Green.—Cloth dyed blue, and well washed, is imbued with the aluminous acetate, dried, and subjected to the quercitron bath.

In the above cases, the cloth, after receiving the mordant paste, is dried, and put through a mixture of cow-dung and warm water. It is then put into the dyeing vat or copper.

DYES FOR BONES AND IVORY.

1. Red.—Made an infusion of Cochineal in water of ammonia, then immerse the pieces therein, having previously soaked them for a few minutes in very weak aquafortis and water.

2. Black.—Immerse the pieces in a weak solution of nitrate of silver, for a short time, then expose them to the sunlight.

3. Green.—Steep in a solution of verdigris, to which a little acquafortis has been added.

4. Yellow.—Boil for one hour in a solution made with one pound of alum in one gallon of water, then take out the pieces and steep them in a decoction made with ½ pound of turmeric in 2 quarts of water, lastly, mix the two liquors, and boil them therein for one hour.

5. Blue.—Stain them green, then steep them in a hot and strong solution of pearlash.

Remarks.—The bones of living animals may be dyed by mixing madder with their food. The bones of young pigeons may thus be tinged of a rose-color in 24 hours, and of a deep scarlet in 3 days; but the bones of adult animals take a fortnight to acquire a rose-color. The bones nearest the heart become tinged quickest. In the same way extract of logwood will tinge the bones of young pigeons purple.

Celebrated Washing Mixture.—Dissolve a half pound of soda in a gallon of boiling water, and pour upon it a quarter pound of lime. After this has settled, cut up 10 ounces of common bar-soap, and strain the solution upon it, and mix perfectly. Great care must be taken that no particles of lime are poured upon the soap. Prepare the mixture the evening before washing.

Directions.—To 10 gallons of water and the above preparation when the water is boiling, and put the clothes in while boiling. Each lot of linen must boil half an hour, and the same liquid will answer for three batches of clothes. The white clothes must be put in soak over night, and if the collars and wristbands are soaped and rubbed lightly, so much the better, Clean cold water may be used for rincing. Some prefer boiling them for a few moments in clean blueing water, and afterwards rince in cold water. The cloths may not appear perfectly white while wet, but when dry will be clear white.

Musk.—Artificial Musk is made by dropping 3½ ounces of nitric acid on one ounce of rectified oil of amber. In a day or two, a black substance is produced, which smells similar to genuine musk.

Mahogany Furniture.—Stains and spots may be taken out of mahogany furniture by the use of a little acquafortis, or oxalic acid and water, by rubbing the part with the liquid, by means of a cork, till the color is restored, observing afterwards to well wash the wood with water, and to dry and polish as usual.

Razor-Paste.—Levigated oxide of tin (prepared putty powder) 1 ounce; powdered oxalic acid, ¼ ounce; powdered gum, 20 grains. Make it into a stiff paste with water, and evenly and thinly spread it over the strop. With very little friction, this paste gives a fine edge to the razor, and its efficiency is still further increased by moistening it.

Shaving-Paste.—White Wax, Spermaceti, and Almond-Oil; melt, and while warm, beat in two square of Windsor soap, previously reduced to a paste with rose-water.

The Hunter's Secret.—To Catch Game—such as Mink, Musk-Rats, Weasels, Raccoons, Otter, etc.—Take one ounce of valerian, ¼ ounce of commercial musk, one pint of whiskey—mix together, and let it stand for two weeks. Put a few drops of this on your bait.

Preservation of Hams.—Most grocers, dealers in hams, and others, who are particular in their meat, usually take the precaution to case each one, after it is smoked, in canvas, for the purpose of defending it from the attacks of the little insect, the dermestes lardarius, which, by laying its eggs in it, soon fills it with its larvæ, or maggots. This troublesome and expensive process may be altogether superseded by the use of pyroligneous acid. With a painter's brush, dipped in the liquid, one man, in the course of a day, may effectually secure two hundred hams from all danger. Care should be taken to insinuate the liquid into all the cracks, etc., of the under surface. This method is especially adapted to the preservation of hams in hot climates.

India-Rubber Blacking.—(*Bryant and James' Paste.*)—Ivory black 60 pounds; treacle 45 pounds; good vinegar and oil of vitriol, of each 12 pounds; India-rubber oil, 9 pounds; mix.

2. *Liquid.*—Ivory black 60 pounds; gum (dissolved), 1 pound; vinegar (No. 24) 20 gallons; oil of vitriol 24 pounds; India-rubber oil, 9 pounds. Mix.

Remarks.—The India-rubber oil is made of caoutchouc 18 oz., dissolved in rape-oil, 9 pounds, by means of heat. The ingredients are mixed together in the same order and manner as common blacking.

Alterative Syrup.—American Sarsaparilla, Yellow Dockroot, Black Alder-bark, Prickly Ash-bark, Burdock-root, Sassafras-bark, Wintergreen, of each one ounce, make four pints of syrup. Dose, a wineglassfull, three or four times a day. This syrup is useful in all diseases where the blood or general system needs purifying.

Bite of a Mad Dog.—Spirits of Hartshorn is said to be a certain remedy for the bite of a mad dog. The wound should be constantly bathed with it, and three or four doses, diluted, taken inwardly, during the day. The hartshorn decomposes chemically the virus insinuated into the wound, and immediately alters and destroys its deleteriousness. The writer, who resided in Brazil for some time, first tried it for the bite of a scorpion, and found that it removed pain and inflamation almost instantly. Subsequently, he tried it for the bite of the rattlesnake, with similar success. At the suggestion of the writer, an old friend and physician tried it in cases of Hydrophobia and always with success.

Canker Powder.—Powdered Golden Seal, Blue Cohosh, of each one ounce. A superior remedy for canker in the mouth and stomach. Steep one teaspoonful of this powder in a gill of hot water for one hour, then strain and sweeten with loaf sugar. Gargle the throat for ten or fifteen minutes at a time with this infusion; likewise a table-spoonful may be held in the mouth for some minutes; after which drink two table-spoonfuls of it. Repeat it several times a day, until a cure is effected.

Cough Candy.—Cheap, Safe, and Excellent.—Take equal parts of Boneset, Spikenard, Elecampane, Comfrey, and Wild Cherry bark; make a strong decoction; to every pint of this decoction add molasses a pint; extract of liquorice, four ounces, and honey four ounces. Boil down to a proper consistence for forming a candy, when add oil of tar, one drachm; essence of sassafras, two teaspoonfuls. Work it up into a candy form by hand in the usual way. It may be eaten freely.

Bronzing of Medals.—Ornaments of copper, electrotypes, etc.— Having thoroughly cleaned and polished the surface of the specimen, with a brush apply the common crocus-powder, previously made into a paste with water. When dry, place it in an iron ladle, or on a common fire-shovel over a clear fire for about one minute; and when sufficiently cool, polish with a plate-brush. By this process a bronze similar to that on tea-urns is produced; the shade depending upon the duration of the exposure to the fire.

1. By substituting finely powdered plumbago for crocus-powder in the above process, a beautiful, deep and permanent bronze appearance is produced.

2. Rub the medal with a solution of livers of sulphur, or sulphuret of potassium, then dry. This produces the appearance of Antique bronze very exactly.

Surface Bronzing.—This term is applied to the process for imparting to the surfaces of figures of wood, plaster of Paris, etc., a metallic appearance. this is done by first giving them a coat of oil or size-varnish, and when this is nearly dry, applying with a dabber of cotton or a camel-hair pencil, any of the metallic bronze powders; or the powder may be placed in a little bag of muslin, and dusted over the surface, and afterwards finished off with a wad of linen. This surface must be afterwards varnished.

Paper is bronzed by mixing the powders up with a little gum and water, and afterwards burnishing.

Iron Castings may be bronzed by thorough cleaning, and subsequent immersion in a solution of sulphate of copper, when they acquire a coat of the latter metal. They must be then washed in water.

Butter or Milk.—To remove its Turnip Flavor. This is said to be removed by either of the following methods: When the milk is strained into the pans, put to every six gallons one gallon of boiling water. Or dissolve one ounce of nitre in a pint of spring water and put ¼ pint to every fifteen gallons of milk.

Silver Jelly.—Time to boil the feet, five hours and a half; to boil the jelly, twenty minutes. One set of calf's feet; one ounce of isinglass; one pint of the best gin; one pound of loaf sugar; juice of six lemons; peel of two; white of six eggs. Boil the calf's feet in four quarts of water, with the isinglass, until the feet are done to rags, and the water wasted to half the quantity; strain it, and when cold remove the feet, and the jelly from the sediment very carefully. Put the jelly into a stew-pan with the sugar, the juice of the lemons, and the peel of two; add the gin. When the flavor is thoroughly drawn from the lemon-peel, put in the whites of the eggs well beaten, and their shells broken up, place the stew-pan over the fire, and let it boil for twenty minutes, but do not stir in after the egg has been added. Dip a jelly-bag into hot water and squeeze it dry; run the jelly through it several times, until quite clear, and then pour it into the mould. If calf's feet cannot be obtained, two ounces of gelatine and one ounce of isinglass will do as well.

Gilding of Porcelain, Glass, etc.—This is performed by blending powdered gold with gum-water and a little borax, and applying it by means of a camel-hair pencil; the article is then heated sufficiently hot in an oven or furnace, by which means the gum is burnt, and the borax vitrifying cements the gold to the surface. When cold it is polished off with a burnisher. Names, dates, or any fancy device may thus be permanently and easily fixed on glass, china, earthenware, etc.

Gilding of Silk, etc.—Silks, satins, woolens, ivory bones, etc., may be readily gilded by immersing them in a solution of nitromuriate (terchloride) of gold (1 of the salt to 3 or 4 water), and then exposing them to the action of hydrogen-gas. The latter part of the process may readily be performed by pouring some diluted sulphuric acid, or zinc or iron filings, in a bottle, and placing it under a jar or similar vessel, inverted at the top of which the articles to be gilded are to be suspended.

The foregoing experiment may be very prettily and advantageously varied as follows: paint flowers or other ornaments with a very fine camel-hair pencil, dipped in the above-mentioned solution of gold, on pieces of silk, satin, etc., and hold them over a Florence flask, from which hydrogen-gas is evolved, during the decomposition of the water by sulphuric acid and iron-filings. The painted flowers, etc., in a few minutes will shine with all the splendor of the purest gold. A coating of this kind will not tarnish on exposure to the air, or in washing.

Gilding Varnish.—This is oil-gilding applied to equipages, picture-frames, furniture, etc., the surface being highly varnished and polished before it receives the size or gold color; and then, after the gilding has become quite dry, a coat of spirit varnish, fumed with the chafing-dish as above, is applied, followed by two or three coats of the best copal varnish, after which the work is carefully polished with tripoli and water.

Gilders' Varnish.—Prep.—Beeswax, 4 ounces, verdigris and sulphate of copper, of each 1 ounce; mix.

Fire-eating.—The power of resisting the action of fire is given to the skin by frequently washing it with diluted sulphuric acid, until the part becomes sufficiently callous. It is said that the following mixture is very efficacious:—dilute sulphuric acid 3 parts; sal ammoniac, 1 part; juice of onions, 2 parts; mix. It is the acid, however, that produces the effect.

Impressions from Coins.—A very easy and elegant way of taking the impressions of medals and coins, not generally known, is as follows.—Melt a little isinglass-glue with brandy, and pour it thinly over the medal, so as to cover its whole surface; let it remain on for a day or two, till it has thoroughly dried and hardened, and then take it off, when it will be fine, clear, and as hard as a piece of Muscovy glass, and will have a very elegant impression of the coin. It will also resist the effects of damp air, which occasions all other kinds of glue to soften and bend if not prepared in this way. (Shaw.) If the wrong side of the isinglass be breathed on, and gold leaf applied, it will adhere, and be seen on the other side, producing a very pleasing effect.

Isinglass-glue, made with water alone, will do "nearly" as well as if brandy be used.

Leaf-gilding.—This term is applied to the gilding of paper, vellum, etc., by applying leaf-gold to the surface, previously prepared with a coating of gum-water, size, or white of an egg. It is usually finished with an agate burnisher.

Letter-gilding. The letters of signboards and similar ornamental gilding for outdoor work, is done by first covering the design with yellow or gold-color paint, then with oil gold size, and when this is nearly dry, applying the leaf-gold, observing to shield it properly from the wind, lest it be blown away or become crumpled before being properly attached. This gilding is usually varnished.

Mahogany Stains.—Pure Socotrine aloes, ounce, dragon's blood, ½ ounce, rectified spirit, 1 pint; dissolve and apply 2 or 3 coats to the surface of the wood, finish off with wax or oil, tinged with alkanet.

Simple Cosmetic.—Soft soap ½ pound; melt over a slow fire with a gill of sweet oil, add half a teacupful of fine sand, and stir the mixture together until cold. The shelly sea-sand, sifted from the shells, has been found better than that which has no shells.

Remarks.—This simple cosmetic, has for several years past been used by many ladies who are remarkable for the delicate softness and whiteness of their hands, which they in a great measure, attribute to the use of it. Its cheapness is a strong recommendation.

Essence of Patchouli.—Indian patchouli-leaves, 2 pounds; rectified spirit of wine, 9 pints; water, a gallon. Macerate for one week, frequently shaking the vessel, then distill over exactly one gallon. A very fashionable perfume.

Essence of Roses. (odorous)—Very fine article.—Attar of roses, 1 ounce; spirit of wine, 1 gallon. Mix in a close vessel, and assist the solution by placing it in a bath of hot water. As soon as the spirit gets warm, take it from the water and shake till quite cold. The next day filter. Unless the spirit of wine be of more than the common strength, it will not retain the whole of the attar in solution in very cold weather.

Furs may be preserved from moths and insects by placing a little colocynth pulp (bitter apples,), or spices, as cloves, pimento, etc., wrapped in muslin among them, or they may be washed in a very weak solution of corrosive sublimate in warm water (10 or 15 grains to the pint), and afterwards carefully dried. Furs, as well as every other species of clothing, should be kept in a clean, dry place.

Coffee Milk.—Boil a dessert-spoonful of ground coffee in about a pint of milk a quarter of an hour; then put into it a shaving or two of isinglass and clear it; let it boil a few minutes, and set it on the side of the fire to fine. This is a very fine breakfast, and should be sweetened with real Lisbon sugar.

Bakers' Itch-ointment.—Mix well together one quarter ounce of ointment of nitrate of mercury and one ounce of balm-oil.

Soap a la Rose.—New Olive-Oil Soap 30 pounds, new tallow soap, 20 pounds; reduce them to shavings by sliding the bars along the face of an inverted plane, melt in an untinned copper pan by the heat of steam or a water-bath, add 1½ ounces of finely ground vermilion. Mix well, remove the heat, and when the mass has cooled a little, add essence of roses [attar?] 3 oz,; do. of cloves and cinnamon, of each, one ounce; bergamot 2½ ounces; mix well, run the liquid mass through a tammy-cloth, and put it into the frames. If the soaps employed are not new, one or two quarts of water must be added to make them melt easily. A very fine article.

Soap au Bouquet.—Best tallow soap, 30 lbs.; essence of bergamot, 4 oz.; oils of cloves, sassafras, and thyme, of each 1 ounce; pure neroli, ½ ounce; finely powdered brown ochre, 7 oz. Mix as last. Very fine.

Soap, Bitter Almond.—Best white tallow soap; ½ cwt.; essence of bitter almonds, 10 oz. Mix as soap a la rose. Very fine.

Soap Cinnamon.—Best tallow soap, 30 pounds; best balm-oil soap, 20 pounds; essence of cinnamon, 7 ounces; do. of sassafras and bergamot, of each 1¼ ounces; finely powdered yellow ochre, 1 pound. Mix as soap a la rose. Very fine.

Soap, Musk.—Best tallow soap, 30 pounds; palm-oil soap, 20 pounds; powdered cloves, pale roses, and gilliflowers, of each, 4½ ounces; essences of bergamot and musk, of each 3½ ounces; Spanish brown, 4 ounces. Mix as soap a la rose. Very fine.

Soap, Orange-flower.—Best tallow soap, 30 pounds; palm-oil soap, 20 pounds; essence of Portugal and ambergris, of each 7½ ounces, yellowish green color [ochre and indigo] 8½ ounces, vermilion, 1¼ ounce. Mix as soap a la rose. Very fine.

Soap, Palm-oil.—Made of palm-oil and caustic soda lye. Has a pleasant odor of violets, and a lively color.

Almond Soap is made from almond-oil and caustic soda, and is chiefly used for the toilet.—Cure Soap is made with tallow and soda. Mottled Soap with refuse kitchen-stuff, etc.

PRINTING INK.

Printing Ink.—10 to 12 gallons of linseed-oil are set over the fire in an iron pot capable of containing at least as much more, to allow of its swelling without running over. When it boils it is kept stirred with an iron ladle, and if it does not take fire of itself soon after the smoke begins to rise, it is kindled by means of a piece of burning paper, stuck in the cleft end of a long stick. The pot is then shortly afterwards removed from the fire, and the oil is suffered to burn for about half an hour, or till a sample of the varnish cooled upon a pallet knife, may be drawn into strings of about half an inch long, between the fingers. The flame is now extinguished by the application of a close-fitting tin cover, and as soon as the froth of the ebullition has subsided, black rosin is added, in the proportion of 6 pounds, to every 6 quarts of oil thus treated; the mixture is next stirred until the rosin is dissolved, when 1¼ lbs. of brown soap, cut into slices is further added (cautiously), and the ingredients are again stirred with the spatula until united, the pot being once more placed over the fire to promote the combination. When this is effected, the varnish is removed from the heat, and after thorough stirring, covered over and set aside. It is necessary to prepare two kinds of this varnish, varying in consistence, from more or less boiling, to be occasionally mixed together as circumstances require; that which answers well in hot weather being too thick in cold, and vice versa. Large characters also require a thinner ink than small ones. A good varnish may be drawn into threads like glue, and is very thick and tenacious.

2,—Making the ink. (Black.) Finely powdered Indigo and Prussian Blue, of each 2½ ounces; best mineral lampblack, 4 pounds; best vegetable lampblack, 3½ pounds; put them into a suitable vessel and mix in gradually the warm varnish. The mixture must now be submitted to careful grinding, either in a mill or with a slab and muller. On a large scale steam power is employed for this purpose.

(An extemporaneous superfine ink). Balsam of copaiba (pure) 9 ounces; lampblack, 3 ounces; Indigo and Prussian Blue, of each, 5 drachms; Indian Red, ¾ ounces; yellow soap (dry), 3 oz., grind to an impalpable smoothness. Canada balsam may be substituted for balsam of copaiba where the smell of the latter is objectionable, but it dries quicker.

Remarks.—Old linseed-oil is preferable to new. Yellow rosin soap is preferred for black and dark-colored inks, and white-cure soap for light ones. Vegetable lampblack takes the most varnish. The addition of Indigo and Prussian Blue is to correct the brown color of the black. The Indian red is added to increase the body and richness of color. Some persons find much trouble in grinding up the indigo, from its running into a mass and clogging the mill; but this may be avoided by mixing it as above, or by first grinding it with sufficient quantity of Canada balsam or copaiba, and using a proportionate quantity of varnish and that of a little thicker consistence. The French employ nut-oil instead of linseed. Mr. Savage obtained the large medal of the Society of Arts for his black ink made as above. It is unrivaled. Colored inks are made in a similar way. The pigments used are, carmine, lake, vermilion, chrome red, red lead, orange red, Indian red, venetian red, orange chrome, chrome yellow, burnt terra di Siena, gallstone, Roman ochre, yellow do., verdigris, Schele's green, Schweinfurth's do., blues and yellows mixed for greens, indigo, Prussian blue, Antwerp do., cobalt do., charcoal do., luster, umber, sepia, etc., etc.

Paper Copying.—Make a stiff ointment with butter or lard and lampblack, and smear it thinly and evenly over soft writing-paper, by means of a piece of flannel, then wipe off the redundant portion with a piece of soft rag. Placed on paper and written on with a style, or solid pen. By repeating the arrangement, two or three copies of a letter may be obtained at once. This paper, set up in a case, forms the ordinary manifold writer.

The Art of Inlaying and Ornamenting Papier-mache. The articles required are a small pair of cutting nippers, a half round file, some gold size, Vegetable Black, Black Japan, two large camel's hair brushes in quills, various powder colors such as Lakes, Vermilion, Italian Pink, Prussian blue, French Ultramarine, Emerald Green, etc. Copal Varnish, Spirit of Turpentine, Gold Leaf, Pumice Stone, Pumice Powder, Putty Powder, Palette Knife and Slab, Papier-mache and Pearl. Having roughly sketched your design upon the Papier-mache, and decided upon the part to be inlaid with Pearl, take your nippers and cut or nip the pearl to your shape, which is afterwards to be finished with the file to the exact form required. You will now mix in a gallipot a small quantity of Gold Size and Vegetable Black, to the consistency of Treacle; and taking a large brush, lay a rather thick coating upon the whole of Papier-mache. You will then stick on the pieces of pearl before cut out, according to your design, and let it remain until dry, which will be 24 hours. The surface of your Papier-mache being perfectly dry, take Black Japan and give it a thick and even coating over the whole surface, not excepting the Pearl. It will require to be placed in an oven of some sort, quite free from dust, and heat about 145 degrees; but this is not particular, so long as it does not get hotter. It will be dry in 24 hours, when to test its dryness, dip a rag in spirit of turpentine, and brush the edge of the papier-mache; if it soils the rag, it is not dry, and requires to be again stoved. The articles require four coats of japan, and the above process to be repeated on each coat, the beauty of the articles entirely depending on the japan being perfectly dry and hard. A piece of pumice-stone, rubbed flat on a flag, must now be dipped in water, and rubbed on the papier-mache until it brings the whole to a level surface, and shows the pearl. Fine pumice powder and water upon a bit of list is now applied to remove the scratches made by the pumice-stone. Polish with putty powder upon a piece of wash-leather.

If your design consists of flowers, etc., color the parts as required with powder colors, mixed up with copal varnish, and diluted with turpentine, using nature as a guide. The ornamental parts, not consisting of flowers, are to be painted and gilded according to your fancy. For gilding, take gold size and mix a little chrome yellow, with which draw your design, and when partially dry in 5 or 10 minutes cut gold leaf in small pieces, apply it, and dab it on with cotton wool. In 5 or 10 minutes after rub the cotton lightly over the surface, to remove the superfluous pieces of gold. When the coloring is dry, varnish over the parts which have been painted or gilded, with copal varnish, and let it dry 24 hours, and the article is complete.

REMEDIES FOR DISEASES OF HORSES.

Laxative Balls (for horses).—Aloes, ginger, and soft soap, of each 3 drachms; mix with treacle for one ball. Cordial and laxative.

Garlic Balls (for horses).—Garlic one ounce; liquorice-powder enough to make a ball. Use for chronic coughs.

Mange Balls (for horses).—Crude antimony, 2 oz.; colomel, 1 oz.; opium, ½ oz.; flowers of sulphur, 1 lb.; mix with treacle and divide into 12 balls. A piece the size of a horsebean to that of a small nut is a capital medicine for dogs.

Stomachic Balls (for horses).—Powdered Gentian, 4 oz.; powdered ginger and carbonate of soda, of each 2 ounces; soft soap, 8 ounces; mix and divide into 8 balls.

Tonic Balls (for horses).—Gentian, ½ oz.; opium, ½ drachm; cascarilla, myrrh, and carbonate of soda, of each, 1 drachm; soft soap, ½ oz. Form into one ball.

Sulphur Balls (for horses).—Flowers of sulphur, 1 pound; powdered antimony, 3 ounces; red sulphuret of mercury (pure), 2 ounces; powdered gum, 1 ounce; treacle to mix. For 12 balls. Said to make the coat slick; also for mange, etc.

Strengthening Balls (for horses).—Powdered calomba and cascarilla, of each ¼ oz.; soft soap, ¾ oz.; chalk, ½ oz.; make into a ball. For looseness.

Worm Balls (for horses).—Aloes, 5 drachms; castile soap, ½ oz.; calomel and ginger, of each, 1½ drachms; oil of cloves and cassia, of each, 6 drops; treacle to make a ball.

Gripe Balls (for horses).—Liquorice, black pepper, ginger, and prepared chalk, all in powder, of each, 4 oz.; oils of caraway, cloves and cassia, each one drachm; treacle to mix. For 12 balls.

Influenza Balls (for horses).—Barbadoes, aloes, nitre, and venice turpentine, of each, 1 pound; gentian, 2 pounds; ginger, ½ pound; treacle to mix. Divide into 1½ ounce balls.

Colic Balls (for horses).—Powdered opium, ¼ oz.; castile soap and camphor, each 1 oz.; powdered ginger and cassia, each ½ oz.; liquorice- powder, 2 oz.; treacle to make 4 balls.

Cordial Balls. (for horses).—Aniseed, caraway-seed, and cumin-seed, of each, 4 pounds; ginger, 2 pounds; all in powder; treacle sufficient to mix. Produce 21 pounds. To be made up in balls weighing 1¾ oz. each.

Cough Balls (for horses).—Cordial ball mass, 4 pounds; gum amoniacum, 4 oz.; powdered squills, 1 oz.; treacle to mix. Divide into 4 dozen balls.

Farcy Balls (for horses).—Corrosive sublimate, 10 grains; liquorice-powder, 1 ounce; oil of aniseed, ½ drachm; mix with treacle for one ball.

Mercurial Balls (for horses).—Calomel, 1 oz.; aloes, 2 oz.; rhubarb, ¾ oz.; liquorice-powder, 14 oz.; treacle to mix. Divide into 12 balls. Laxative and alterative.

Alterative Balls (for horses).—Calomel, sulphuret of antimony, and powdered opium, of each, ½ oz.; powdered gum guaiacum, 2½ ounces; castile soap, 12 ounces; treacle to mix. Divide into 12 balls. Use for weak horses with a bad constitution.

2. Calomel, ½ oz.; powdered aloes, 1½ oz.; starch, 6 oz.; soft soap, 8 oz. Make them into a mass, and divide into 12 balls. Use to improve the constitution.

The Arabian Charm for Taming Horses.—The horse castor is a wart or excrescence which grows on every horse's fore-legs, and generally on the hind-legs. It has a peculiar rank, musty smell, and is easily pulled off. For the Oil of Cumin the horse is said to have an instinctive passion, and the Oil of Rhodium possesses some very peculiar properties for animals. Produce some horse castor and grate it fine—also get some Oil of Rhodium and Oil of Cumin, and keep the three separate in air-tight bottles. Rub a little Oil of Cumin upon the hand, and approach the horse in the field on the windward side, so that he can smell the Cumin—when he approaches, immediately rub your hand gently upon the horse's nose, getting a little oil on it. Then give him a little of the castor on a piece of loaf sugar, apple, or potato. Then put eight drops of the Oil of Rhodium into a lady's silver thimble.

—Take the thimble between the thumb and middle finger of your right hand, with the forefinger stopping the mouth of the thimble, to prevent the oil from running out whilst you are opening the mouth of the horse. As soon as you have opened the horse's mouth, empty the thimble upon his tongue and he is your servant.

Artificial Yeast.—Honey, 5 oz.; cream of tartar, 1 oz.; malt, 16 oz.; water at 122° F. 3 pints; stir together, and when the temperature falls to 65°, cover it up and keep it at that temperature till yeast is formed.

To Attract Rats.—Two drachms of oil of aniseed, two drops of nitrous acid, and two grains of musk. Oil of Rhodium is also supposed to be very attractive to these vermin. Assafœtida with these oils is also used.

Rheumatism.—Take two eggs, one gill of vinegar, one gill of New England Rum, one teaspoonful of spirits of turpentine, one teaspoonful of sunfish-oil. Beat the eggs up well first, then add a small quantity of each article at a time, until all are mixed, stirring the mixture all the time. Bathe the affected parts with it two or three times a day.

British Herb Tobacco.—The principal ingredient in this compound is dried coltsfoot leaves, to which a portion of thyme, wood-betony, eyebright, and rosemary are added.

Hair Depilatory.—Quicklime, 16 ounces; pearlash 2 ounces; liver of sulphur, 2 ounces. Reduce to a fine powder, and keep in a close bottle. To be mixed with water, and applied to the skin, and scraped off in three or four minutes with a wooden knife. [Use caution, to prevent injury.]

Dupuytren's Pomade.—Beef-marrow, 6 oz.; nervine balsam, 2 oz. "This is made by melting together 4 oz. each of beef-marrow and oil of mace, and adding 2 dr. of balsam of tolu, and 1 dr. each of oil of cloves and camphor, dissolved in ½ oz. of rectified spirit." Peruvian balsam, 2 oz.; oil of almonds, 1½ oz.; extract of cantharides 16 gr. Melt the marrow and nervine balsam with the oil, strain, add the balsam of Peru, and lastly the extract, dissolved in a drachm of rectified spirit.

Rouge.—Rouge is prepared from carmine, and the coloring matter of safflower, by mixing them with finely levigated French chalk or talc, generally with the addition of a few drops of olive or almond oil. Sometimes fine white starch is used as the reducing ingredient.

Hair-dye.—Nitrate of silver, 11 drachms; nitrate acid, 1 drachm; distilled water, 1 pint; sap green, 3 drachms; gum arabic, 1 dr. Mix.

Hair-dye.—Litharge, 2 parts; slaked lime, 1 part; chalk, 2 parts; all finely powdered, and accurately mixed. When required for use, mix the powder with warm water, and dip a brush in the mixture, and rub the hair well with it. After two hours let the hair be washed.

Toothache.—Opium, 5 gr.; oil of cloves, 3 drops; extract of henbane, 5 gr.; extract of belladonna, 10 gr.; powdered pellitory sufficient to form a paste.

Rose Tooth-paste.—Cuttlefish-bone, 3 oz.; prepared or precipitated chalk, 2 oz.; orris, 1 oz.; lake or rose pink to give it a pale rose color, otto of rose, 16 drops; honey of roses in sufficient quantity.

Filling for Teeth.—Gutta-percha, softened by heat, is recommended. Dr. Rollfs advises melting a piece of caoutchouc at the end of a wire, and introducing it while warm.

Fictitious Gold.—Platina, 7; copper, 16; zinc, 1. Fuse together.

Common Gold.—Copper, 16; silver, 1; gold, 2.

Bailey's Itch-ointment.—Olive-oil, 1 lb.; suet, 1 lb.; alkanet-root, 2 oz. Melt, and macerate until colored; then strain, and add 3 oz. each of alum, nitre, and sulphate of zinc, in very fine powder, adding vermilion to color it, and oil of aniseed, lavender, and thyme to perfume.

Caustic for Corns.—Tincture of iodine, 4 dr.; iodide of iron, 12 gr.; chloride of antimony, 4 dr. Mix, and apply with a camel-hair brush, after paring the corn. It is said to cure in three times.

Consumption.—Rum, ½ pint; linseed-oil, honey, garlic (beaten to a pulp), and loaf sugar, of each 4 oz., yolks of 5 eggs. Mix. A teaspoonful night and morning.

Sweet's Salve.—Melt together 8 ounces of rosin and 2 ounces of beeswax; then add the following mixture in powder; bole armenia, nitre, camphor, of each one ounce. Stir them well together, then pour the whole into cold water, and work it in the water until it can be taken out and formed into rolls or cakes.

Opodeldoc.—White soap, 2 ounces; camphor, 1 ounce; oil of rosemary, 2 drachms; oil of origanum, 2 drachms; strong aqua ammonia, 1 ounce; proof alcohol, 1½ pints. Dissolve together.

Infants' Cordial.—Pleurisy-root, scull-cap, skunk-cabbage, hops, cramp-bark, prickly-ash berries, calamus, angelica seed, sassafras, of each, in powder, one ounce; ginger, capsicum, of each two drachms. Pour on six pints of boiling water: When cold, add three pints of good Holland Gin, and two pounds of loaf-sugar. Let it stand two weeks, frequently shaking. [We have substituted this for Godfrey's, as it is far superior.]

Milk of Roses.—Mix one ounce of fine olive-oil with 10 drops of oil of tartar, and a pint of rose-water.

Macassar-oil.—The oil made by the natives in the islands is obtained by boiling the kernel of the fruit of a tree resembling the walnut, called in Malay, *Badeau*. The oil is mixed with other ingredients, and has a smell approaching to that of creosote. But the Macassar-oil sold in this country has probably no relation to the above, except in name. The following is given by Gray: Olive-oil, 1 pound; oil of origanum, 1 drachm. Others add 1¼ drachms of oil of rosemary.

Eau d'Ange.—Flowering tops of myrtle, 16 oz.; rectified spirit, a gallon; digest, and distill to dryness in a water-bath; or dissolve ¼ ounce essential oil of myrtle in three pints of rectified spirit. Mr. Gray gives under this name a water without spirit: water, 2 pints; benzion, 2 ounces; storax, 1 ounce; cinnamon, 1 drachm; cloves, 2 drachms; calamus, a stick; coriander-seeds, a pinch. Distill.

Russian Tooth-powder.—Peruvian-bark, 2 oz.; orris-root, 1 oz.; sal ammoniac, ½ ounce; catechu, 6 dr.; myrrh, 6 dr.; oil of cloves, 6 or 8 drops.

Beetle Poison.—Put a drachm of phosphorus in a flask with 2 ounces of water; plunge the flask into hot water, and when the phosphorus is melted pour the contents into a mortar with 2 or 3 ounces of lard. Triturate briskly, adding water, and ½ pound of flour with 1 or 2 ounces of brown sugar.

Cockroach Poison.—Equal parts of Plaster of Paris, with oatmeal.

Arsenical Paste.—Melt 2 pounds of suet in an earthen vessel over a slow fire, and add 2 pounds of wheat flower, 3 ounces of levigated white arsenic, 2½ drachms of lampblack, 15 drops of oil of aniseed. It may be used alone, or mixed with bread, crumbs, etc. For destroying rats and mice.

Washes for Vermin in Plants.—Infuse one pound of tobacco in a gallon of boiling water, in a covered vessel, till cold.

For Lice in Vines,—Boil ½ pound of tobacco in 2 quarts of water; strain, and add ½ pound of soft soap, and ¼ pound of sulphur. Mix.

For Aphides.—Boil 2 oz. of lime and 1 oz. of sulphur in water, and strain.

For Red Spiders.—A teaspoonful of salt in a gallon of water. In a few days wash the plant with pure water.

To Mark on Glass.—Glass may be written on for temporary purposes, by French chalk; pencils of this substance will be found convenient. Glass may be written on with ink, if the surface be clean and dry, and the pen held nearly perpendicular.

The shellac ink is the best for labels, as it resists damp, etc. "To scratch glass," a scratching diamond is used, or a piece of flint, or crystal of quartz, or the point of a small three square file. "To engrave on glass," fluoric acid is used, either in the liquid state or in vapor. The glass must be warmed, and coated with wax or engravers' cement, and the writing or design traced through the wax with a bradawl or other pointed instrument. The liquid fluoric acid is poured on it, and left to act on the uncovered portions of the glass; or the fluor-spar may be powdered and made into a paste with oil of vitriol, and laid over the prepared surface, and covered with lead-foil or tea-lead: or bruised fluor-spar is put on a Wedgewood evaporating basin, with sufficient oil of vitriol to form a thin paste, and the prepared glass laid over the basin, so that the vapors may act on the portions from which the wax has been removed. "To cut glass," (besides the usual method of dividing cut glass by a glaziers diamond), the following means may be used: To divide glass tubes or rods, form a deep mark around them with the edge of a three square file: then with a hand placed on either side of the mark, break the rod with a slightly stretching as well as bending motion. A diamond or sharp flint may be substituted for a file. Flasks, globes, and retorts, may be divided by means of iron rings, having a stem fixed in a wooden handle. Make the ring red-hot, and apply it to the flask, etc. If the vessel does not break where it came it contact with the ring, wet the part, and it will generally separate. Another method is to twist together 2 or 3 threads of cotton, such as is used for wicks: moisten them with spirit of wine, and encircle the flask with them; then, holding the flask horizontally, set fire to the wick, and turn the flask with the fingers, so as to keep the flame in the direction of the thread. If the separation does not take place the first time, the process may be repeated after the glass has cooled. By these means a common oil-flask may be divided into an evaporating dish and a funnel. By means of a stout iron rod, fixed in a wooden handle, and terminating in a blunt point and heated to redness, broken retorts, globes, and flasks, may be converted into useful evaporating dishes, etc. If any crack exists, it may easily be led in any direction, as it will follow the motion of the heated iron. If no crack exists one must be produced by applying the point of the heated rod to any convenient spot on the edge of the broken glass, touching it afterwards with a moistened finger, if necessary. The edges of glass thus divided are rendered less apt to break by heating them in the flame of a blowpipe, or grinding them smooth with emery on a flat stone.

To Silver Glass.—The term "silvering" is applied to the process of coating the surface of glass with amalgamated tin foil, in forming mirrors. The tinfoil is rubbed over with quicksilver, and more of the latter poured over it; the plate of glsss, perfectly clean and dry, is then applied to it in such a way as to exclude all air-bubbles, and to bring the glass and foil into perfect contact. The plate, after being inclined so as to allow the superfluous quicksilver to drain off, is loaded with weights, under which it remains till the adhesion is complete. To convex and concave mirrors, the amalgamated foil is applied by accurately fitting plaster moulds. The interior of globes is silvered by introducing a liquid amalgam, and turning about the globe till every part is covered with it. But a method of literally silvering glass has lately been patented by Mr. Drayton. He mixes 1 oz. of nitrate of siver, 3 oz. of water, 1 ounce of liquid ammonia, and 3 oz. of spirit of wine, and filter the solution after it has stood 3 or 4 hours. To every ounce of solution he adds ¼ oz. of sugar (grape sugar, if possible,) dissolved in equal quantities of water and alcohol. The surface to be silvered is covered with this liquid, and a temperature of 160° F. maintained, till the deposition of the silver is complete. When quite dry, the coated surface is covered with mastic varnish.

Cement for Steam Pipes.—Good linseed-oil varnish, ground with equal weights of white lead, oxide of manganese, and pipeclay.

Inks.—The following are specimens of the most useful kinds of ink:—

Black Writing-ink.—Bruised Aleppo galls, 6 oz.; soft water, 6 pints. Boil together, add 4 oz. of sulphate of iron, and 4 oz. of gum arabic. Put the whole in a bottle, and keep it in a warm place, shaking it occasionally. In two months pour it off into glass bottles, and add to each pint a grain of corrosive sublimate, or 3 or 4 drops of creosote. Add one ounce of brown sugar to the above, and it will make good copying ink.

Blue Ink.—Prepare a solution of iodide of iron from iodine, iron, and water; add to the solution half as much iodine as first used, pour this solution into semi-saturated solution of ferro-prussiate of potash, containing nearly as much of the salt as the whole weight of iodine. Collect the precipitate, wash it, and finally dissolve it in water, to form the blue ink. The solution from which the precipitate is separated, evaporated to dryness, and the residue fused, re-dissolved and crystalized, yields pure iodide of potassium. This process is patented.

Gold and Silver Ink.—Fine bronze-powder, or gold, or silver leaf, ground with a little sulphate of potash, and washed from the salt, is mixed with water, and a sufficient quantity of gum.

Ink for Marking Linen.—Nitrate of silver, 100 grains; distilled water, 1 ounce; gum arabic, 2 drachms; sap green, a scruple. Dissolve. The linen is first to be wetted with the following "pounce," dried and rubbed smooth, then written on by a clean quill or bone pen dipped in the ink. Pounce: Subcarbonate of soda, 1 ounce; water, 8 ounces.

Indelible Ink.—Take 20 parts of Dantzig potash, 10 of tanned leather parings, and 5 of sulphur; boil them in an iron pot with sufficient water to dryness; then raise the heat, stirring the matter constantly, till the whole becomes soft, taking care that it does not ignite. Add sufficient water, and filter through cloth. It must be kept from the air. It resists many chemical agents.

Cement for Glass, China, etc.—Isinglass, one ounce; distilled water, 6 ounces; boil to 3 ounces, and add 1½ ounces of rectified spirit. Boil for a minute or two, strain, and add, while hot, first ½ ounce of a milky-emulsion of ammoniac, and then 5 dr. of tincture of mastic. [There are various kinds of this cement sold, and some of the improvements introduced have not been made public..]

Coppersmiths' Cement.—Powdered quicklime, mixed with bullock's blood, and applied immediately.

Gilding.—Leaf-gold is affixed to various surfaces, properly prepared by gold size, or other adhesive medium. Metallic surfaces are coated with gold by means of amalgam of gold and mercury, applied with a wire brush, wet with an acid solution of mercury, made by dissolving 10 parts of mercury in 11 of nitric acid, by a gentle heat, and adding 2½ parts of water. The article thus coated is heated over charcoal till the mercury is dissipated, and afterwards burnished. To give it a redder color, it is covered with gilder's wax (a compound of verdigris, ochre, alum, and yellow wax), again exposed to heat, and afterwards washed and cleaned by a scratch-brush and vinegar. An inferior kind of gilding is effected by dissolving gold, with a fifth of its weight of copper, in nitro-muriatic acid, dipping rags in the solution, drying and burning them, and rubbing the ashes on the metallic surface with a cork dipped in salt and water.

Electro Gilding is thus performed:—A solution of 5 oz. of gold is prepared and boiled till it ceases to give out yellow vapors; the clear solution is mixed with 4 gallons of water, 20 pounds of bicarbonate of potash added, and the whole boiled for two hours. The articles, properly cleaned, are suspended on wires, and moved about in the liquid from a few seconds to a minute, then washed, dried, and colored in the usual way. The solution used in gilding with the voltaic apparatus is made by dissolving ¼ ounce of oxide of gold with 2 ounces of cyanide of potassium, in a pint of distilled water.

Balls for Cleaning Clothes.—Bathbrick, 4 parts; pipeclay, 8 parts; pumice, 1; soft-soap, 1; ochre, umber, or other color, to bring it to the desired shade, sufficient ox-gall to form a paste. Make into balls, and dry them.

To Stain Wood a Mahogany Color (*dark*).—Boil one pound of madder and 2 ounces of logwood in a gallon of water, and brush the wood well over with the hot liquor. When dry, go over the whole with a solution of 2 drachms of pearlash in a quart of water.

To Strain Maple a Mahogany Color.—Dragon's blood, ½ ounce; alkanet, ¼ ounce; aloes, 1 drachm; spirit of wine, 1¼ ounces. Apply it with a sponge or brush.

Rosewood.—Boil 8 ounces of logwood in 3 pints of water until reduced to half; apply it boiling hot two or three times, letting it dry between each. Afterwards put on the streaks with a camel-hair pencil dipped in a solution of copperas and verdigris in decoction of logwood.

Ebony.—Wash the wood repeatedly with a solution of sulphate of iron; let it dry, then apply a hot decoction of logwood and nutgalls for two or three times. When dry, wipe it with a wet sponge, and polish with linseed-oil.

French Polish.—Orange shellac, 22 ounces; rectified spirit 4 pints; dissolve.

Etching Fluids (for steel).—Mix 10 parts of pure hydrochloric acid, 70 of distilled water, and a solution of 2 parts of chlorate of potash in 20 of water. Dilute before using with from 100 to 200 parts of water. *(For Copper)*—Iodine, 2 parts; iodide of potassium, 5 parts; water, 5 to 8 parts.

Silvering Compound.—Nitrate of silver, 1 part; cyanide of potassium (Liebig's) 3 parts; water sufficient to form a thick paste. Apply it with a rag. A bath for the same purpose is made by dissolving 100 parts of sulphate of soda, and 15 of nitrate of silver, in water and dipping the article to be silvered into it.

Tracing Paper.—Paper well wetted with Canada balsam and camphine, and dried.

Shampoo Liquor.—Rum, three quarts; spirit of wine, one pint; water, one pint; tincture of cantharides, ¼ ounce; carbonate of ammonia, ½ ounce; salt of tartar, 1 ounce. Rub it on and afterwards wash with water. By omitting the salt of tartar it nearly resembles the balm of Columbia.

Waterproof Compound.—Suet, 8 ounces; linseed-oil, 8 ounces; yellow beeswax, 6 ounces; neatsfoot oil, 1½ ounces; lampblack, 1 oz., litharge ½ oz. Melt together, and stir till cold.

Kittoe's Lotion for Sunburns, Freckles, etc.—Muriate of ammonia, 1 drachm sprin water, a pint; lavender water, 2 drachms. Apply with a sponge 2 or 3 times a day.

Virgin's Milk.—Simple tincture of benzoin, 2 drachms; orange-flower water, 8 ounces. It may be varied by using rose or elder-flower water.

Coloring for Brandy, etc.—Sugar melted in a ladle till it is brown, and then dissolved in water or lime-water.

Colors for Liquors.—Pink is given by cochineal, yellow by saffron or safflower, violet, by litmus, blue, by sulphate of indigo, saturated with chalk; green by the last, with tincture of saffron, or by sap-green.

To Preserve Butter.—Powder finely, and mix together, 2 parts of the best salt, one of loaf-sugar, and one of nitre. To each pound of butter, well cleansed from the milk, add one oz. of this compound. It should not be used under a month. [Butter that has an unpleasant flavor is said to be improved by the addition of 2½ drachms of bicarbonate of soda to 3 pounds of butter. A turnipy flavor may be prevented by only feeding the cows with turnips immediately after milking them.]

To Preserve Eggs.—Jayne's liquid (expired patent) is thus made: Take a bushel of lime, 2 pounds of salt, ½ pound of cream of tartar, and water enough to form a solution strong enough to float an egg. In this liquid it is stated, eggs may be preserved for two years.

How to make Fly-poison.—A common poison for flies consists of white arsenic or king's yellow, with sugar, etc., but the use of such compounds may lead to fatal accidents. A sweetened infusion of quassia answers the same purpose, and is free from danger. Pepper, with milk, is also used; and also some adhesive compounds, by which they are fatally entangled.

Indian Ink.—Real lampblack, produced by combustion of linseed-oil, ground with gum, and infusion of galls. It is prepared both in a fluid and solid form, the latter being dried in the sun.

Bedbug Poison.—Scotch snuff mixed with soft soap.

Sympathetic or Secret Ink.—[The solutions used should be so nearly colorless that the writing is not seen till the agent is applied to render it visible.]

1. Digest 1 oz. of taffre, or oxide of cobalt, at a gentle heat,

with 4 oz. of nitro-muriatic acid till no more is dissolved, then add one oz of common salt, and 16 oz. of water. If this be written with and the paper held to the fire, the writing becomes green, unless the cobalt should be quite pure, in which case it will be blue. The addition of a little nitrate of iron will impart the property of becoming green. It is used in chemical landscapes for the foliage.

3. Boil oxide of cobalt in acetic acid. If a little common salt be added, the writing becomes green when heated; but with nitre it becomes a pale rose-color.

6. A solution of sulphate—or preferably, persulphate—of iron. It becomes black when washed with infusion of galls; BLUE, by prussiate of potash. [This constitutes colorless ink, which becomes visible when written with on paper containing galls, or tannin, or prussiate of potash.]

Fattening Calves.—Aniseed, ¼ pound; fenugrec, ¼ pound; linseed meal 1 pound. Make it into a paste with milk, and cram them with it.

Blake's Toothache Remedy.—Finely powdered alum, 1 drachm; spirit nitric ether, 7 drachms.

British Oil.—Oil of turpentine, and linseed oil, of each 8 ounces; oil of amber, and oil of Juniper, of each 4 ounces; true Barbadoes tar, 3 ounces; American Petroleum, 1 ounce. Mix.

To Preserve Milk.—Milk the cow into glass bottles, and seal them to keep out the air.

Armenian Cement.—Soak isinglass in water till soft; then dissolve it in proof spirit; add a little Galbanum or gum Ammoniac, and mix it with tincture of mastic. It must be kept well stopped, and when wanted, liquefied by the phial being immersed in hot water. Used to cement jewels upon watch cases; to mend china, or to replace leaves torn out of books.

To Prevent Flies from Setting on Pictures, Picture Frames, or other Furniture.—Soak a large bundle of Leeks for five or six days in a pail of water, and then wash or sponge the pictures, etc., over with it.

To Cure Butter.—Take 2 parts of the best common salt, 1 part of sugar, and one part of saltpetre. Beat them up, and mix well together. Take one ounce of this to every pound of butter, work it well into a mass, and close it up for use. Butter thus cured, appears of a rich marrowy consistence and fine color, and does not acquire a brittle hardness, nor taste salt. It will keep good for three years, if let stand three or four weeks before opening it.

Wash to Whiten the Nails.—Take diluted sulphuric acid, 2 dr.; pump water, 4 ounces; Tincture of myrrh, 1 drachm. Mix. First cleanse with white soap, and then dip the fingers into the wash.

To join Glass together.—Take a little isinglass, and melt it in spirits of wine. It will form a transparent glue, which will unite glass, so that the fracture will be almost imperceptible. The greatest care is necessary, that the spirits of wine shall not boil over into the fire.

To Renovate old Apple-trees.—Take fresh made lime from the kiln; slake it well with water, and well dress the tree with a brush, and the insects and moss will be completely destroyed.

The outer ring will fall off, and a new, smooth, clean, healthy one formed, and the trees assume a most healthy appearance, and produce the finest frui

To prevent the Smoking of a Lamp.—Soak the wick in strong vinegar, and dry it well before you use it. It will then burn both sweet and pleasant, and give much satisfaction for the trifling trouble in preparing it.

To make Silvering Powder.—Get from a drug-store 1 oz. of what is called Hydrargirum, *Cum Creta*, and mix it with 4 oz. prepared chalk. Used to give a silver polish to brass, copper, britannia ware, etc. To be rubbed on with a dry cloth.

Nerve Ointment.—Take half a pint of neatsfoot-oil, one gill of brandy, one gill of spirits of turpentine, and simmer them together fifteen minutes. Excellent for sprains, swellings, and rheumatism.

To Free Plants from Leaf-lice.—Mix 3 ounces of flowers of sulphur with a bushel of sawdust. Scatter this over the plants infested with these insects, and they will soon be freed, though a second application may possibly be necessary.

Strawberry Jelly.—Take of the juice of strawberries, 4 pounds; sugar, 1 pound. Boil to a jelly.

To Avoid Injury from Bees.—A wasp or a bee swallowed may be killed before it can do harm, by taking a teaspoonful of common salt dissolved in water. It kills the insect, and cures the sting. Salt at all times is the best cure for external stings. Sweet-oil, pounded mallows, onions, or powdered chalk made into a paste with water, are also efficacious. If bees swarm up on the head, smoke tobacco, and hold an empty hive over the head, and they will enter it.

How to Make Rose-water—Take half an ounce white sugar, and drop into it 2 or 3 drops of otto of rose; then grind very fine in a mortar. After it is well ground into fine powder, pour on it half a pint of cold water; grind well for a few moments, and then mix it all with one gallon of cold water. Let it stand for 3 or 4 days, and strain through fine muslin.

Whitewashing.—A pint of varnish mixed with a bucket of whitewash will give it, in a great degree, the qualities of paint; and it will withstand all kinds of weather.

Nankin Dye.—Take arnotto and prepared Kali, equal parts, boiled in water; the proportion of Kali is altered, as the color is required to be deeper or lighter. Used to restore the color of faded nankin clothing, or to dye new goods of a nankin color.

To make Spice Bitters.—Golden Seal, Poplar-Bark, Bayberry, bark of the root, Sassafras, bark of the root. of each one pound; Unicorn-root, Bitter-root, Cloves, Capsicum, of each, 4 ounces, Loaf-sugar, 4 pounds. Put to one ounce of this powder, one quart of sweet wine; let it stand a week or two before using it. Dose—a wineglassful two or three times a day.

How to make Saur Kraut.—Take a large strong wooden vessel, or cask, resembling a salt-beef cask, and capable of containing as much as is sufficient for the winter's consumption of a family. Gradually break down or chop the cabbages (deprived of outside green leaves) into very small pieces; begin with one or two cabbages at the bottom of the cask, and add others at intervals, pressing them by means of a wooden spade, against the side of the cask, until it is full. Then place a heavy weight on top of it and allow it to stand near a warm place, for four or five days. By this time it will have undergone fermentation, and be ready for use. Whilst the cabbages are passing through the process of fermentation, a very disagreeable fetid, acid smell, is exhalted from them. Now remove the cask to a cool situation, and keep it always covered up. Strew aniseed among the layers of the cabbage during its preparation, which communicates a peculiar flavor to the Saur Kraut at an after period. In boiling it for the table, two hours is the period for it to be on the fire. It forms an excellent, nutritious, and antiscorbutic food, for winter use.

Bedbugs.—A strong decoction of ripe red pepper is said to be as efficacious an antidote to bedbugs as can be selected from the multitudinous recipes for the purpose.

Burning-Fuid.—Take four quarts of alcohol and one quart of spirits of turpentine. Mix well together.

To Extract Paint from Cotton, Silk, and Woolen Goods.—Saturate the spots with spirits of turpentine, and let it remain several hours; then rub it between the hands. It will crumble away, without injuring the color or texture of the article.

To make Silver-Plating Powder. for silvering brass, copper, etc., and for repairing worn-out parts of plated goods.—Nitrate of silver, 30 grains; common table-salt, 30 grains; cream of tartar, 3½ drachms. Mix all thoroughly, and make into a fine powder in a mortar. Moisten a soft cloth, dip into the powder, and rub over the surface to be plated for a few moments; then wash off with a solution of common salt in water, and rub dry with a cloth and chalk or whiting.

To make Violet or Purple Ink.—Boil 16 ounces of logwood in 3 quarts of rain water, to three pints; then add 3 ounces of clean gum arabic and 5 ounces of alum (powdered). Shake till well dissolved. It would be well to strain through a wire sieve.

To Clean Kid Gloves.—Add 15 drops of strongest solution of ammonia to spirits of turpentine ½ pint. Having fitted the gloves on wooden hands or pegs, apply this mixture with a brush. Follow up this application with some fine pumice powder. Rub with some flannel or sponge dipped in the mixture. Rub off the sand, and repeat the same process twice or thrice. Hang in the air to dry, and, when dry, place in a drawer with some scent.

To make Matches without Sulphur or Phosphorus.—Chlorate of potash, separately powdered, 6 drachms; vermilion, 1 drachm; lycopodium, 1 drachm; fine flour, two drachms. Mix carefully the chlorate with the flour and lycopodium, avoiding *much friction*, then add the vermilion, and mix the whole with a mucilage made with one drachm of powdered gum arabic, 10 grains of tragacanth, 2 drachms of flour, and 4 ounces of hot water. Mix. Add sufficient water to bring it into a proper consistence, and dip in the wood previously dipped in a solution of one ounce of gum camphor, in six ounces of oil of turpentine,

To make Black Ink Powder.—Sulphate of copper [bluestone], one ounce; gum arabic, 2 ounces; green vitriol [copperas], 8 oz.; nutgalls, powdered, 1 pound; extract of logwood, 1 pound. All are to be finely pulverized. About one ounce of this mixture will be required to make one pint of ink, to be put into boiling water. It should stand about two weeks before using.

Baking Powder.—Baking soda, 6 ounces; cream tartar, 8 ounces. Each should be thoroughly dry before mixing. About a teaspoonful, dissolved in warm milk or water is sufficient for a quart of flour.

To make Syrup of Sarsaparilla,—Take of sarsaparilla-root, 1 lb.; boiling water, 5 quarts; sugar, 1 pound. Cut or chop up the sarsaparilla-root into short pieces, the shorter the better, put it into the water, let it stand for 24 hours, then boil down to 2½ quarts, and strain the liquid *while hot*. Then add the sugar, and boil gradually for about an hour. When cool, put into bottles or a jug, and keep corked. Dose, from one to two tablespoonfuls before each meal. This is a valuable medicine to *purify the blood*, and is used with great advantage in all cases of general debility or weakness from any cause whatever: also, for disease of the liver, dyspepsia, or indigestion, scrofula, female weakness, loss of appetite, effects of syphilis or venereal disease, and in every case where the wish is to *build up* and *strengthen* the system. It should be used about two months or more at a time.

To Make Medicated Root-beer.—For each gallon of water to be used, take hops, burdock, yellow dock, sarsaparilla, dandelion, and spikenard roots, bruised, of each ½ ounce; boil about 20 minutes; and strain while hot; add 8 or ten drops of oils of spruce and sassafras, mixed in equal proportion. When cool enough not to scald your hand, put in two or three tablespoonfuls of yeast; molasses: two-thirds of a pint, or white sugar ½ pound, gives it about the right sweetness. Keep these proportions for as many gallons as you wish to make. You can use more or less of the roots to suit your taste, after trying it. It is best to get the dry roots, or dig them and let them dry, and of course you can add any other root known to possess medicinal properties desired in beer. After all is mixed let it stand in a jar with a cloth thrown over it, to work about two hours, then bottle and set in a cool place. This is a nice way to take alteratives, without taking medicines to operate on the bowels.

To Make Ice Cream.—Fresh cream, ½ gallon; rich milk, ½ gallon; white sugar one pound. Dissolve the sugar in the mixture, and flavor with extract to suit your taste; or take the peel from a fresh lemon and steep one half of it in as little water as you can, and add this. It makes the lemon flavor better than the extract, and no flavor will so universally please as the lemon. Keep the same proportion for any amount desired. The juice of strawberries or raspberries gives a beautiful color and flavor to ice-creams; or about ½ oz. of essence or extracts to a gallon, or to suit the taste. Have your ice well broke; one quart salt to a bucket of ice. About half an hour's constant stirring, and an occasional scraping down and beating together, will freeze it.

Ice-Cream (a cheaper kind).—Milk, 6 quarts; Oswego cornstarch, ½ pound. First dissolve the starch in one quart of the milk, and then mix all together and just simmer a little (not to boil). Sweeten and flavor to suit your taste, as above.

Chicago Plan of making Ice-Cream.—Irish moss, 1½ ounces; milk, one gallon. First soak the moss in a little cold water for an hour, and rinse it well to clear it of sand and a certain peculiar taste; then steep it for an hour in the milk just at the boiling point, but not to boil. It imparts a rich color and flavor without eggs or cream. The moss may be steeped *twice*. A few minutes rubbing, at the end of freezing, with the spatula against the side of the freezer, gives ice-cream a smoothness not otherwise obtained, and makes it look nice.

To Make Fever and Ague Pills.—Quinine, 20 grains; Dovers-powders, 10 grains; sub-carbonate of iron, 10 grains. Mix with mucilage of gum arabic, and make into 20 pills. Dose: two every hour, beginning four or five hours before the chill is expected. When the chills have been broken, take one pill night and morning for a month, to prevent a return.

To Make Axle-Grease.—One pound of black lead ground fine and smooth with four pounds of lard. A little powdered gum-camphor is sometimes added.

To Tan Raw Hide.—When taken from the animal spread it flesh side up; then put 2 parts of salt, 2 parts of saltpetre and alum combined, make it fine, sprinkle it evenly over the surface, roll it up, let it alone for a few days until dissolved; then take off what flesh remains, and nail the skin to the side of a house in the sun; stretch it tight. To make it soft like harness leather, put neatsfoot oil on it. Fasten it up in the sun again: then rub out all the oil you can with a wedge-shaped stick, and it is tanned with the hair on.

To make Refined Oil for Watches, Sewing-machines, etc.—Take sweet-oil, 1 pint, put into a bottle and then put into the oil 2 oz. of thin sheet-lead, in coils. Set the bottle where it will be exposed to the sun for a month (shaking it up once a week); then strain through a fine wire or cloth sieve, and keep tightly corked.

How to Make Transparent Soap.—Slice 6 pounds of nice bar soap into thin shavings, put into a brass, tin, or copper kettle, with 2 quarts of alcohol, and heat it gradually over a slow fire, stirring till all the soap is dissolved; then add one ounce of sassafras, and stir till all is mixed. You will then pour into pans 1½ inches deep; and, when cold, cut into bars or cakes as may be desired.

To Make Self-raising Flour.—This is made by adding 4 pounds of the following mixture to every 100 pounds of flour, and then mixing all completely. It must be kept perfectly dry, and, in using, mix quickly and *put into the oven at once.* Here is the mixture referred to above: carbonate of soda, 56 pounds, tartaric acid, 28 pounds, potato-flour, 112 pounds. Having used bread made from self-raising flour, we can testify that it is good.

To make Solid Candles from common Lard.—Dissolve ¼ lb. of alum and ¼ lb. saltpetre in ½ pint of water on a slow fire; then take 3 lbs. of lard, cut into small pieces, and put into the pot with this solution, stirring it constantly over a very moderate fire until the lard is dissolved; then let it simmer until all steam ceases to rise, and remove it at once from the fire. If you leave it too long it will get discolored. These candles are harder and better than those made from tallow.

How to Make Oroide Gold.—Spanish copper, 16 parts; silver, 4 parts; gold, 1 part. Melt together.

To make Renovating Mixture. for removing grease-spots, etc.—

Aqua-ammonia, 2 ounces; soft water, 1 quart; saltpetre, 1 teaspoonful; variegated soap, 1 ounce. Mix all, shake well, and it will be a little better to stand a few hours or days before using, which gives the soap a chance to dissolve.

Directions.—Pour upon the place a sufficient amount to well cover any grease or oil which may get spilled or daubed upon coats, pants, carpets, etc., sponging and rubbing well, and applying again if necessary to saponify the grease in the garment; then wash off with clear cold water.

To make Magic Copying or Impression or Duplicating Paper.—To make black paper, lampblack mixed with cold lard. Red paper, venetian red mixed with lard. Blue paper, prussian blue mixed with lard. Green paper, chrome green mixed with lard. The above ingredients to be mixed to the consistencey of thick paste, and to be applied to the paper with a rag or brush; then take a flannel rag and rub till the color ceases coming off. Cut your sheets 4 inches wide and 6 inches long; put 8 sheets together, 2 of each color, and sell for 25 cents per package.

Directions for Writing with this Paper.—Lay down your paper upon which you wish to write, then lay on the copying paper, and over this lay any scrap of paper you choose; then take any hard-pointed substance, and write as you would with a pen. To take impressions of flowers, leaves, etc., press them between this paper and a sheet of clean white paper, and then lay the leaf on another clean sheet of paper, and press the paper gently over it.

S. & S. MANUAL LIBRARY.

No. 1—THE ALBUM WRITER'S ASSISTANT.
No. 2—THE WAY TO DANCE.
No. 3—THE WAY TO DO MAGIC.
No. 4—THE WAY TO WRITE LETTERS.
No. 5—HOW TO BEHAVE IN SOCIETY.
No. 6—AMATEUR'S MANUAL OF PHOTOGRAPHY.
No. 7—OUT-OF-DOOR SPORTS.
No. 8—HOW TO DO BUSINESS.
No. 9—THE YOUNG GYMNAST.
No. 10—THE HUNTER AND ANGLER.
No. 11—SHORT-HAND FOR EVERYBODY.
No. 12—THE TAXIDERMIST'S MANUAL.

For sale by all Booksellers and Newsdealers, or will be sent, POSTAGE FREE, to any address in the United States or Canada, on receipt of price, 10 cents each, by the publishers.

THE HAND=BOOK LIBRARY

No. 1—WOMEN'S SECRETS; or, How to be Beautiful. . . . 25c

Nos. 2-3—TITLED AMERICANS. . 50c

No. 4—SELECT RECITATIONS AND READINGS. . . . 25c

No. 5—ZOLA'S FORTUNE-TELLER. 25c

These popular books are large type editions, well printed, well bound, and in handsome covers. For sale by all Booksellers and Newsdealers; or sent, postage free, on receipt of price, by the publishers,

STREET & SMITH,

P. O. Box 2734. 25 to 31 Rose Street, New York.

THE PRIMROSE SERIES

OF

WORLD'S BEST FICTION,

Comprising translations of the best foreign fiction, together with the works of popular **English and American Authors.**

ISSUED SEMI-MONTHLY.   PRICE, 50 CENTS.

No. 1—ANOTHER MAN'S WIFE,
By Bertha M. Clay............ 50
No. 2—THE BELLE OF THE SEASON,
By Mrs. Harriet Lewis........ 50
No. 3—DOCTOR JACK,
By St. George Rathborne...... 50
No. 4—KATHLEEN DOUGLAS,
By Julia Truitt Bishop.......... 50
No. 5—HER ROYAL LOVER,
By Ary Ecilaw................ 50
No. 6—JOSE,
By Otto Ruppius........... 50
No. 7—HIS WORD OF HONOR,
By E. Werner................ 50
No. 8—A PARISIAN ROMANCE,
By A. D. Hall................ 50

THE PRIMROSE SERIES combines the highest art of bookmaking with the best fiction that can be obtained. For sale by all Booksellers and Newsdealers; or sent, postpaid, on receipt of price, by

STREET & SMITH, PUBLISHERS,

P. O. BOX 2734.   25-31 ROSE STREET, NEW YORK.

THE SELECT SERIES
OF
POPULAR AMERICAN COPYRIGHT STORIES.

No. 60—WON ON THE HOMESTRETCH, by Mrs. M. C. Williams 25
No. 59—WHOSE WIFE IS SHE? by Annie Lisle 25
No. 53—KILDHURM'S OAK, by Julian Hawthorne 25
No. 57—STEPPING-STONES, by Marion Harland 25
No. 56—THE DAUGHTER OF THE REGIMENT, by Mary A. Denison 25
No. 55—ROXY HASTINGS, by P. Hamilton Myers 25
No. 54—THE FACE OF ROSENFEL, by C. H. Montague 25
No. 53—THAT GIRL OF JOHNSON'S, by Jean Kate Ludlum 25
No. 52—TRUE TO HERSELF, by Mrs. J. H. Walworth 25
No. 51—A BEAUTIFUL WOMAN'S SIN, by Hero Strong 25
No. 50—MARRIED IN MASK, by Mansfield Tracy Walworth 25
No. 49—GUILTY OR NOT GUILTY, by Mrs. M. V. Victor 25
No. 48—THE MIDNIGHT MARRIAGE, by A. M. Douglas 25
No. 47—SADIA THE ROSEBUD, by Julia Edwards 25
No. 46—A MOMENT OF MADNESS, by Charles J. Bellamy 25
No. 45—WEAKER THAN A WOMAN, by Charlotte M. Brame 25
No. 44—A TRUE ARISTOCRAT, by Mrs. Georgie Sheldon 25
No. 43—TRIXY, by Mrs. Georgie Sheldon 25
No. 42—A DEBT OF VENGEANCE, by Mrs. E. Burke Collins 25
No. 41—BEAUTIFUL RIENZI, by Annie Ashmore 25
No. 40—AT A GIRL'S MERCY, by Jean Kate Ludlum 25
No. 39—MARJORIE DEANE, by Bertha M. Clay 25
No. 38—BEAUTIFUL, BUT POOR, by Julia Edwards 25
No. 37—IN LOVE'S CRUCIBLE, by Bertha M. Clay 25
No. 36—THE GIPSY'S DAUGHTER, by Bertha M. Clay 25
No. 35—CECILE'S MARRIAGE by Lucy Randall Comfort 25
No. 34—THE LITTLE WIDOW, by Julia Edwards 25
No. 33—THE COUNTY FAIR, by Neil Burgess 25
No. 32—LADY RYHOPE'S LOVER, by Emma G. Jones 25
No. 31—MARRIED FOR GOLD, by Mrs. E. Burke Collins 25
No. 30—PRETTIEST OF ALL, by Julia Edwards 25
No. 29—THE HEIRESS OF EGREMONT, by Mrs. Harriet Lewis 25
No. 28—A HEART'S IDOL, by Bertha M. Clay 25
No. 27—WINIFRED, by Mary Kyle Dallas 25
No. 26—FONTELROY, by Francis A. Durivage 25
No. 25—THE KING'S TALISMAN, by Sylvanus Cobb, Jr 25
No. 24—THAT DOWDY, by Mrs. Georgie Sheldon 25
No. 23—DENMAN THOMPSON'S OLD HOMESTEAD 25
No. 22—A HEART'S BITTERNESS, by Bertha M. Clay 25
No. 21—THE LOST BRIDE, by Clara Augusta 25
No. 20—INGOMAR, by Nathan D. Urner 25
No. 19—A LATE REPENTANCE, by Mrs. Mary A. Denison 25
No. 18—ROSAMOND, by Mrs. Alex. McVeigh Miller 25
No. 17—THE HOUSE OF SECRETS, by Mrs. Harriet Lewis 25
No. 16—SYBIL'S INFLUENCE, by Mrs. Georgie Sheldon 25
No. 15—THE VIRGINIA HEIRESS, by Mrs. May Agnes Fleming 25
No. 14—FLORENCE FALKLAND, by Burke Brentford 25
No. 13—THE BRIDE-ELECT, by Annie Ashmore 25

These popular books are large type editions, well printed, well bound, and in handsome covers. For sale by all Booksellers and Newsdealers; or sent, *postage free*, on receipt of price, 25 cents each, by the publishers,

STREET & SMITH,

P. O. Box 2734.   25 to 31 Rose Street   New York.

The Secret Service Series.

No. 36—THE GREAT TRAVERS CASE, by Dr. Mark Merrick.
No. 35—MUERTALMA; OR, THE POISONED PIN, by Marmaduke Dey.
No. 34—DETECTIVE BOB BRIDGER, by R. M. Taylor.
No. 33—OLD SPECIE, by Alexander Robertson, M. D.
No. 32—ADVENTURES AND EXPLOITS OF THE YOUNGER BROTHERS, by Henry Dale.
No. 31—A CHASE ROUND THE WORLD, by Mariposa Weir.
No. 30—GOLD-DUST DARRELL, by Burke Brentford.
No. 29—THE POKER KING, by Marline Manly.
No. 28—BOB YOUNGER'S FATE, by Edwin S. Deane.
No. 27—THE REVENUE DETECTIVE, by Police Captain James.
No. 26—UNDER HIS THUMB by Donald J. McKenzie.
No. 25—THE NAVAL DETECTIVE'S CHASE, by Ned Buntline.
No. 24—THE PRAIRIE DETECTIVE, by Leander P. Richardson.
No. 23—A MYSTERIOUS CASE, by K. F. Hill.
No. 22—THE SOCIETY DETECTIVE, by Oscar Maitland.
No. 21—THE AMERICAN MARQUIS, by Nick Carter.
No. 20—THE MYSTERY OF A MADSTONE, by K. F. Hill.
No. 19—THE SWORDSMAN OF WARSAW, by Tony Pastor.
No. 18—A WALL STREET HAUL, by Nick Carter.
No. 17—THE OLD DETECTIVE'S PUPIL, by Nick Carter.
No. 16—THE MOUNTAINEER DETECTIVE, by Clayton W. Cobb.
No. 15—TOM AND JERRY, by Tony Pastor.
No. 14—THE DETECTIVE'S CLEW, by "Old Hutch."
No. 13—DARKE DARRELL, by Frank H. Stauffer.
No. 12—THE DOG DETECTIVE, by Lieutenant Murray.
No. 11—THE MALTESE CROSS, by Eugene T. Sawyer.
No. 10—THE POST-OFFICE DETECTIVE, by Geo. W. Goode.
No. 9—OLD MORTALITY, by Young Baxter.
No. 8—LITTLE LIGHTNING, by Police Captain James.
No. 7—THE CHOSEN MAN, by Judson R. Taylor.
No. 6—OLD STONEWALL, by Judson R. Taylor.
No. 5—THE MASKED DETECTIVE, by Judson R. Taylor.
No. 4—THE TWIN DETECTIVES, by K. F. Hill.
No. 3—VAN, THE GOVERNMENT DETECTIVE, by "Old Sleuth."
No. 2—BRUCE ANGELO, by "Old Sleuth."
No. 1—BRANT ADAMS, by "Old Sleuth."

For sale by all Booksellers and Newsdealers, or will be sent, POSTAGE FREE, to any address in the United States or Canada, on receipt of price, 25 cents each, by the publishers,

STREET & STREET,

P. O. Box 2734.   25 to 31 Rose Street, New York.

THE SEA AND SHORE SERIES.

Stories of Strange Adventure Ashore and Afloat.

No. 23—BUFFALO BILL'S BEST SHO , by Ned Buntline.
No. 22—THE STRUGGLE FOR MAVERICK, by J. F. I1 ls.
No. 21—ROCKY MOUNTAIN SAM, by Burke Brentford.
No. 20 - THE HOUSE OF SILENCE, by Dr. J. H. Robinson.
No. 19—THE IRISH MONTE CRISTO'S TRAIL, by Alex. Robertson, M. D.
No. 18 - THE YANKEE CHAMPION, by Sylvanus Cobb., Jr.
No. 17—FEDORA, from the famous play of the same name, by Victorien Sardou.
No. 16—SIBALLA, THE SORCERESS, by Prof. Wm. H. Peck.
No. 15—THE GOLDEN EAGLE, by Sylvanus Cobb, Jr.
No. 14—THE FORTUNE-TELLER OF NEW ORLEANS, by Prof. Wm. H. Peck.
No. 13—THE IRISH MONTE CRISTO ABROAD, by Alex. Robertson, M.D.
No. 12—HELD FOR RANSOM, by Lieut. Murray.
No. 11—THE IRISH MONTE CRISTO'S SEARCH, by Alex. Robertson, M. D.
No. 10—LA TOSCA, from the celebrated play, by Victorien Sardou.
No. 9—THE MAN IN BLUE, by Mary A. Denison.
No. 8—BEN HAMED, by Sylvanus Cobb, Jr.
No. 7—CONFESSIONS OF LINSKA.
No. 6—THE MASKED LADY, by Lieutenant Murray.
No. 5—THEODORA, from the celebrated play, by Victorien Sardou.
No. 4—THE LOCKSMITH OF LYONS, by Prof. Wm. H. Peck.
No. 3—THE BROWN PRINCESS, by Mrs. M. V. Victor.
No. 2—THE SILVER SHIP, by Lewis Leon.
No. 1—AN IRISH MONTE CRISTO.

For sale by all Booksellers and Newsdealers, or will be sent, POSTAGE FREE, to any address in the United States or Canada, on receipt of price, 25 cents each, by the publishers,

STREET & SMITH,

P. O. BOX 2734. 25-31 ROSE STREET, NEW YORK.

A FIRST-CLASS PAPER FOR BOYS AND GIRLS.

ISSUED WEEKLY.   PRICE 5 CENTS PER COPY.

Stories are constantly running through the columns of GOOD NEWS from the pens of

WM. H. THOMES,	CAPTAIN MACY,
OLIVER OPTIC,	W. B. LAWSON,
HORATIO ALGER, Jr.,	Lieut. LOUNSBERRY,
GEO. H. COOMER,	M. QUAD,
CHAS. BARNARD,	Lieut. JAS. K. ORTON,
JAMES OTIS,	MAX ADELER,
EDWARD S. ELLIS,	"FRANK," Author of
HARRY CASTLEMON	"Smart Aleck."

The illustrations and typographical appearance of GOOD NEWS are in keeping with the high literary merit of its contents. We aim to produce

The Best Weekly of the Times for Boys and Girls,

and, by virtue of our long experience, we have won for GOOD NEWS the first place in the popular favor of all young Americans.

We will send you No. 1 to No. 10 GOOD NEWS, inclusive, for 10 cents, as samples.

STREET & SMITH, Publishers,

P. O. Box 2734.   25 to 31 Rose Street, New York.

www.ingramcontent.com/pod-product-compliance
Lightning Source LLC
Chambersburg PA
CBHW020146170426
43199CB00010B/902